Merry Christmas M.J.

Our Friend, B. Daniel
                Dec. 25, 1995

Herb Carneal writes the same way he broadcasts—with a depth of clarity and a classic touch of humor. Hi Everybody! *is a must read for all true baseball fans.*
—Ernie Harwell

Three words describe Herb: Professional, Professional, Professional. I've had the pleasure of working with Herb over the years. He makes it easy, fun, enjoyable—major league in every way. Thanks, Herb.
—Tom Kelly

As a partner on Twins broadcasts, Herb Carneal is a Hall of Famer. As a friend, he's like my brother.
—Frank Quilici

Like Harm, Tony, Rod, and Kirby, Herb Carneal is Twins baseball.
—Gene Mauch

Hi Everybody!

Herb Carneal

with Stew Thornley

NODIN PRESS
Minneapolis

ISBN: 0-931714-69-9

Nodin Press, a division of Micawber's, Inc.
525 North Third Street
Minneapolis, MN 55401

Dedication

It has been my intention that if I ever attempted to do a book, I would dedicate it to the fans. Not only have they been very nice to me over the years, but imagine that over three million of them came to the Metrodome in 1988 to watch the Twins. Once in a while I wonder if the fans are taken for granted, but without them there certainly would be no spectator sports such as baseball. I never want to forget the shut-ins, so many of whom have told me that a special part of their day is our Twins broadcast.

Also, I want to thank my family, Kathy, Terri, and my mother, for their encouragement and understanding during my 40 years as a major-league baseball announcer. The baseball season makes for an upside-down schedule. While some families may be enjoying long weekends at the lake, going on vacations or participating in other summertime events, our family has had to contend with a never-ending baseball season each summer. There are times when we arrive home from a road trip at the airport at three o'clock in the morning. Kathy is usually there to meet me. My family's willingness to adapt to this kind of schedule has been a tremendous help.

Contents

The Twins had a day for me in 1991. It's nice to be reminded every so often that what you do is appreciated. *WCCO Radio*.

Preface

Baseball lends itself to radio.

People aren't hanging on every pitch. They don't have to keep their eyes glued to a television screen, and they don't have to keep their ears tuned in to a radio either. Baseball is played during the summer, when people are out doing other things. People enjoy radio broadcasts while sitting in a boat or working in a garden. During the summer they'd rather listen to the radio on the porch than watch television cooped up indoors.

This is especially true in Minnesota and the surrounding states, where we don't get much summer. Baseball fans often write and mention their activities, such as milking cows, while listening to a baseball game.

And just when I'm wondering, "Why am I doing this?" I receive a card from a shut-in or from somebody in a nursing home.

The cards and letters were especially valuable to me in the summer of 1993, when I underwent a major heart operation to replace a valve. When I woke up after the operation, the first person I saw was my wife, Kathy, and the first words out of my mouth were, "Hi everybody!" That may seem like a strange way of greeting my wife, but "Hi everybody!" is the phrase I use to open my baseball broadcasts. Through the years it's become more than a greeting: it's an expression that everything's all right, there's baseball on the way, and what more could anyone want. I still had a long period of re-covery ahead of me, but the time passed quickly, thanks to the response of the fans: boxes and boxes and boxes of let-ters and cards.

I tried to answer all of them. I started handwriting re-sponses. Then a friend of mine, Rick Doll, helped with his computer. It's easy to say, "Maybe I'll send a card," and then forget about it, but so many people wrote personal notes, and some of the cards were homemade. They helped me get back doing the games a little ahead of schedule.

During a half-century of broadcasting various sports, mostly baseball, I've seen a lot of great moments, and all those moments have been shared with the fans. This book is about what I've seen and the people I've met during my years as a sportscaster, to relive some of those moments and once again share them with the fans.

Part One

Oriole and Viking Time

My parents, Charles and Edith Carneal

Southern Comfort

I was born on May 10, 1923 in Richmond, Virginia, and didn't exactly grow up in the lap of luxury. My father, Charles, was not in good health. He was in and out of hospitals before he passed away when I was seven years old, at the start of the great Depression. Fortunately, my mother, Edith, had a job as a milliner, and we made do, the two of us. My grandmother, my mother's mother, also lived with us for a while, and I probably spent as much time with her as with my mother.

Richmond had been the capital of the Confederate States of America during the War Between the States, and many battles were fought in Virginia. We visited the battlefields of Fredericksburg and Manassas and also went to places like Appomattox and Williamsburg, but I was never a great student of history. Richmond was still a very segregated city when I was growing up, although I never gave the matter much thought. A black youngster, around my age, hung around with my friends and me all through elementary and junior-high school, and played baseball and football with us just like anybody else.

For as long as I can remember, I was crazy about baseball, which was something I got from my mother. She was a remarkable woman and eventually lived with Kathy and me right up to the time she passed away in 1990 at the age of 98. Right up to the end she was pretty self-sufficient, although we usually liked to have someone be with her when we were gone. Once Dick Doll, a family friend (and now our son-in-law), offered to stay with her. He was running a little late, though, and Kathy and I had to leave before he arrived. In between, my mother decided to make some pork chops. Her cooking set off the smoke alarm but my mother, who was hard of hearing, didn't pay any attention to it and just kept cooking those pork chops. A few minutes later, Dick Doll pulled up at the same time the fire engines were arriving. He rushed in, wondering what was the matter, and found my mother in the kitchen. "Oh, Dick," she said, "I'm glad you're here. Will you see if you can find out what that infernal noise is?" She was quite a character.

Most of the sports I played as I grew up were on the sandlot and weren't too organized, although I did play some American Legion baseball. I was a pitcher and center fielder. My fastball wouldn't have broken a pane of glass. But I had a few different pitches, and I did have good control and rarely walked anybody. For me, pitching was timing: throwing the hitter's timing off so he couldn't get the fat part of the bat on the ball. I could run and catch the ball, so on the days when I didn't pitch I was out in center field. I was never much of a hitter. Overall, I was decent, but I played with some fellows who went into pro ball, and they had far more baseball talent.

For some reason John Marshall High School in Richmond didn't have a baseball team. They had an excellent football team, but by then I was no longer interested in football. I started working when I was in high school, so I didn't have much time for sports. By my senior year, I had arranged my schedule so I'd be done with classes at 12:30, and I worked at the Imperial Tobacco Company from 1:00 to 5:00 every afternoon, running errands, typing—whatever they asked me to do. There wasn't time for baseball, but I played softball after work.

My mom earned enough money making hats that we weren't poor as I was growing up, although we were a long way from rich. My mom and I went to semipro baseball games on weekends. They didn't charge an admission, but midway through the game a hat was passed around for a "silver offering," as they called it, and some of the spectators would toss in nickels and dimes and, once in a while, even a quarter. Sometimes we went to a game of the Richmond Colts, a minor-league team, Class B in the Piedmont League. In those days the classifications for the minor leagues ranged from Class D, at the lowest level, to C, B, A, Double-A, and Triple-A. At the time I started following baseball, the Colts were unaffiliated with a major-league team. Soon after, it became typical for a minor-league team to be owned or controlled by a major-league "parent" for the purpose of developing talent for that major-league team. In the 1930s, the minors were the place for young players working their way up to the majors and were also a haven for older players who no longer could perform at the major-league level. Today, a major-league player can retire in good financial shape, but in the 1930s and 1940s a lot of guys went back to the minors because they couldn't afford to retire and baseball was their only skill. Even though the Colts were an independent team, they had an informal agreement with the New York Giants, who sent players to Richmond for more seasoning. Class B was a long way from the majors, but a few Colts made it to the big leagues: pitchers Monte Kennedy and Tom Ferrick, first baseman Babe Young, and outfielder Buster Maynard.

During the time I was growing up, the Piedmont League had teams in North Carolina and Virginia: the Charlotte Hornets, who eventually had a working agreement with the

Washington Senators; the Asheville Tourists, a St. Louis Cardinals' farm club; the Durham Bulls, a farm team for the Cincinnati Reds; the Rocky Mount Red Sox, affiliated with the Boston Red Sox; the Winston-Salem Twins, who had a working agreement with the Detroit Tigers; the Norfolk Tars, a Yankee farm team; the Newport News Shipbuilders, a farm team for the Brooklyn Dodgers; and the Portsmouth Cubs, who weren't affiliated with the Chicago Cubs or any other team. Around 1940 the first big "bonus baby" from the Piedmont League was signed by the Detroit Tigers: Dick Wakefield, who had played for the Winston-Salem Twins. Wakefield had a nice career in the majors, mostly with the Tigers, and finished with a lifetime batting average of .300.

Another outstanding alumnus of the Piedmont League is Hall of Fame pitcher Early Wynn, who pitched with Charlotte in the late 1930s and early 1940s and then won 300 games in the majors. I got to know him when he was a pitching coach for the Minnesota Twins. He grew up in the little town of Hartford, Alabama. In 1937, when he was 17 years old, he heard that the Washington Senators were about to have a try-out camp in Sanford, Florida. He didn't have enough money for bus fare, so he hitchhiked all the way to Sanford, tried out, and received a contract from the Senators. Early spent 23 years in the big leagues and appeared in 693 games, winning 300 and losing 244. He helped pitch two teams into the World Series: the Cleveland Indians in 1954, when he went 23-11 in wins and losses, and the light-hitting Chicago White Sox in 1959, when he won 22 and lost 10. He was no slouch as a switch-hitting batter with a career batting average of .286.

If Early were pitching today, he might have some problems. He was mostly a high-ball pitcher, and now umpires are reluctant to call strikes when the pitch is above the belt. Also, Early was not averse to giving a message pitch to a batter who was acting too aggressively at the plate. He told me about pitching to Gil McDougald, the Yankees' shortstop, shortly after McDougald had been called up by the Yankees. McDougald stepped into the batter's box and asked the umpire for time and started digging in. Early was set to pitch, but McDougald kept digging and digging so he could really anchor that back foot. Early started walking in toward McDougald.

When he was about halfway to the plate, McDougald said, "It's okay. I'm ready."

Early replied, "I don't know about that. I don't think you dug that hole near deep enough."

Another player I well remember from the Piedmont League was left-handed pitcher Johnny Vander Meer, who was with the Durham Bulls. He was a hard thrower without much control. One night in a game against the Colts he beaned our left-handed-hitting outfielder, Ray Scantling, and Scantling never played another game. There was no such thing as a batting helmet in those days. Vander Meer went up to the Reds in 1937 and the following year pitched two straight no-hitters. In his next start, he didn't allow a hit until the fourth inning and ended up with a three-hitter. In three consecutive starts, he allowed three hits. Vander Meer's second no-hitter was against the Dodgers in the first night game ever played in Brooklyn, when the artificial lighting wasn't as good as it is now. Facing a hard-throwing pitcher without very good control is never easy for a batter, and with such weak lighting the batter was naturally reluctant to get much of a foothold in the batter's box. Despite that one outstanding stretch in 1938, Vander Meer retired with a good but not great record.

Tom Ferrick, after pitching with the Richmond Colts, went on to a career with the Philadelphia Athletics, Cleveland Indians, Washington Senators, St. Louis Browns, and

New York Yankees. Then he became a major-league scout. I ran into him once when he was scouting and asked him about his playing days in Richmond, especially about travel in those days. For a remote team like Richmond a trip to a game in Asheville, North Carolina, was more than 400 miles down through the Smokey Mountains with no freeways, when the buses weren't as comfortable as they are today. But Ferrick said, "We had the best travel of any team in the Piedmont League because our owner, Eddie Mooers, also owned a Packard automobile agency in Richmond and let us travel in limousines."

Back when I was following the Colts, they played at Tate Field on Mayo Island, adjacent to a Naval Reserve Armory and the Virginia Boat Club, with the James River right behind the left-field fence. The left-field line was only around 280 feet, so a lot of home runs, as well as long fouls, went into the water, and Eddie Mooers stationed somebody in a rowboat out on the James to retrieve those balls hit into the river. About every other year a spring flood would inundate the park, and the Colts transferred some of their games to the Richmond City Stadium. At Tate Field, one player hit a tremendous home run that not only cleared the center-field fence but landed on a railroad trestle well beyond. That player was Babe Ruth, playing there in a New York Yankees exhibition game in the 1930s.

Tate Field was the site of a nasty scene after a game between the Colts and Charlotte Hornets, managed by Calvin Griffith, who later owned the Minnesota Twins. As Charlotte players were boarding their team bus, some fans, who had apparently had too much to drink, yelled insults at them. Calvin said something to the rowdies, and they grabbed him and dragged him toward the railing of the railroad bridge, acting as though they intended to throw him over. Fortunately, Early Wynn, a Charlotte pitcher at the

18

time, reached into his equipment bag, pulled out his spikes, and went after those fellows, who let Calvin go and took off.

Tate Field burned down in 1941, and the team moved into a new park in Richmond called Mooers Field, named after the owner. The city of Richmond still has minor-league baseball. They now play in the Class Triple-A International League, are a farm team of the Atlanta Braves, and are known as the Richmond Braves. I've never seen a game at their home stadium, The Diamond, but supposedly it's one of the better minor-league parks.

Although locally we had only semi-pro and minor-league teams, my friends and I developed loyalties to the Washington Senators. In 1939, when I was 16, I went to Washington with some friends to see the Senators play the Boston Red Sox. Griffith Stadium, the Senators' home park, was much bigger than any stadium I had seen before. In a way, it was the reverse of Boston's Fenway Park, which has a high wall in left field. At Griffith Stadium, the right-field wall was high, over 40 feet high. My friends and I figured a player would really have to get the fat part of the bat on the ball to lift it high enough to clear that wall. Although batters hitting toward left field wouldn't have to contend with a high fence, they had to deal with the long distance: 405 feet down the left-field line. Obviously, this was not the place to go if you wanted to see home runs, and a few years later, the Senators hit only one home run all season at Griffith Stadium, an inside-the-park homer by Joe Kuhel.

In the game my friends and I saw, the Senators were leading, 2-0, in the sixth inning, when it started to rain. Play was suspended, and after about an hour and a half, the umpires came back out, looked the field over, said it was unplayable, and called the game. The Senators had won, 2-0—we thought. But the Washington grounds crew was in a dispute with the front office and had refused to put the tarpaulin on the infield when time was called because of the rain. If they had rolled out the tarpaulin, the game could possibly have been resumed when the rain let up. Joe Cronin, the Red Sox manager, protested the umpires' ruling, and the American League president, Will Harridge, decided that the Senators had been responsible for covering the infield with a tarpaulin, and Harridge awarded the game to the Red Sox on a forfeit. Ironically, Cronin was an in-law of the Griffith family, the owners of the Senators: Cronin's wife, Mildred, was the sister of Calvin Griffith. (She must have felt torn whenever the Senators and Red Sox played.)

Even though the nearby Senators were the natural team to follow, I had another favorite team, the St. Louis Cardinals in the National League. There were many stories about that bunch, called the Gashouse Gang—the Dean brothers, Paul and Diz, the team's top pitchers, and Pepper Martin and Joe "Ducky" Medwick and Frankie Frisch, the player-manager. Some members of the Gashouse Gang formed a band called the Mississippi Mudcats. My favorite player was the Cardinal left fielder, Joe Medwick, who is now in the Hall of Fame. Medwick collected almost 2,500 hits in his career, had a lifetime batting average of .324, and appeared in 12 World Series games, hitting .326 in those games. Two-base hits were his specialty, and his total of 64 doubles in 1936 is still a National League record. In the seventh game of the 1934 World Series the Cardinals had a big lead over the Detroit Tigers when Medwick slid hard into Tiger third baseman Marv Owen. When Ducky Joe took his position in left field, Tiger fans pelted him with all sorts of debris, and the baseball commissioner, Judge Kenesaw Mountain Landis, ordered Medwick removed from the game. The Cardinals won, 11-0, with Dizzy Dean pitching the shutout. After the game when Medwick was asked about the barrage he had received in left field, he replied, "I'm not surprised the

Detroit fans threw all that stuff at me. What I can't figure out is why they brought it in the first place."

Although I never met Joe Medwick, I did talk once with the great third baseman of the Gashouse Gang, Pepper Martin, at an exhibition game that was rained out. Pepper hung around afterward, and I said it was too bad that the game had been rained out. Pepper said, "Well, I guess some of the fans here are disappointed, but, you know, the rain was kind of nice too, because the flowers need it, the trees need it, and the grass needs it. And don't all those things look beautiful after a nice rain like we had today." As we continued our conversation, he said he often received more money in the World Series than during the regular season. When the Cardinals sent him his travel money to come to training camp in the spring, he would save it and, believe it or not, hop a freight train to spring training in St. Petersburg.

Later, in 1942, I saw the Cardinals play a couple of World Series games against the New York Yankees. The Cardinals were no longer the Gashouse Gang, and Medwick, Martin, and Dean were long gone, although St. Louis had other great players such as Enos Slaughter and Stan Musial. The series opened with two games in St. Louis. The Yankees, heavy favorites to win the series, took the first game, 7-4. Red Ruffing of the Yankees had a no-hitter until Terry Moore singled with two out in the eighth. The Cardinals won the second game, 4-3, and the series shifted to New York for the next three games.

My friends and I, along with 70,000 other fans, were in Yankee Stadium for the third game, which was a great pitching duel between Ernie White of the Cardinals and New York's Spud Chandler. The Cardinals held a 1-0 lead through much of the game, with a lot of help from their outfielders. In the last of the sixth, with two out and a runner on, Joe DiMaggio of the Yankees hit a long drive toward the

21

gap in left-center field. Center fielder Terry Moore made a diving catch to save at least a run. Many agree that Moore's catch was one of the best ever made in a World Series. In the next inning, the other two Cardinal outfielders got into the act. Stan Musial reached into the left-field seats to rob Joe Gordon of a home run. Then, on the very next play, Enos Slaughter leaped in front of the right-field fence and took a home run away from King Kong Keller. Those big plays kept the Cardinals in front by a run until the ninth, when they scored again and ended up winning, 2-0.

We didn't have tickets for the fourth game, which the Cardinals won, 9-6. We were back at Yankee Stadium for the fifth game, a pitching matchup between Johnny Beazley and Red Ruffing, who had come so close to no-hitting the Cardinals in the first game. Game Five was tied, 2-2, in the top of the ninth, when Whitey Kurowski, the Cardinals' third baseman, hit a two-run homer into the left-field seats. In the last of the ninth, though, the Yankees got their first two batters on base, but Cardinal catcher Walker Cooper snuffed their rally when he threw down to shortstop Marty Marion to pick Joe Gordon off second base. Beazley then retired the next two batters. The Cardinals had won the World Series.

As a kid, I was like most of my friends, crazy about baseball and other sports. Maybe I was a little crazier than most. By the time I graduated from high school, I had decided that I wanted to spend my life in sports, but I had realized early on that it wouldn't be as a player. There were other ways to be involved, and I would find them.

Learning the Trade

Right after graduating from high school I got a job broadcasting for WMBG Radio in Richmond. I opened the station at six in the morning and did mostly booth announcing, giving station identifications and the time and temperature between shows. I didn't have my own show, but it was a start, and there was always the chance that something might open up with sports.

Late at night as I was growing up, I'd turn my radio dial, trying to pick up a broadcast of a baseball game from anywhere. Sometimes I listened to Bob Elston covering the Cubs games on WCFL in Chicago, and sometimes I could get the Yankees. I wondered, "How in the world do you get a job like that—sitting there telling everybody what's going on down on the field." Years later, I learned how Ray Christensen, one of my broadcast partners with the Minnesota Twins, had honed his skills. As a boy, Ray and his friends played dice baseball games, and Ray did the announcing. I did the same growing up in Richmond. My friends and I made up our own games with certain combinations of the dice indicating a single, a strike out, and so on. We formed teams with lineups of players' cards from packs of bubble gum, which cost only a penny or two in those days. We even kept statistics. We devised dice games for all sports, even boxing, and whatever the sport was, I did the broadcasting, calling out the play-by-play the dice dictated.

Soon after I started at the Richmond radio station, our regular sports announcer, Jack Hooper, became ill and couldn't broadcast a boxing match. The station manager knew I followed sports and asked if I could handle the assignment. "I don't know," I said. "I'll try." It went okay, and I started thinking more about broadcasting sports as a career.

One day, I spotted an ad in *Broadcasting Magazine* for a job at a radio station in Syracuse, New York. I sent an audition tape, and they liked it. In 1945, I went to work at WSYR Radio in Syracuse. They already had a full-time sports announcer, and I broadcast football games for Watertown High School, about 70 miles from Syracuse. When WSYR added an FM station and acquired the rights to basketball games at Syracuse University, I worked my way into that.

Occasionally, I broadcast re-creations of major-league games. As the details of the game came in on a Western Union ticker, I gave the play-by-play in the studio just as though I was watching the game. Re-creating games is now a lost art, but in those days stations across the country covered all kinds of sports this way.

I did some sportscasting in person, for the Syracuse Nationals, who played in the National Basketball League. The Nationals had a good team, but they weren't world-beaters. Their best player was Dolph Schayes, who's now in the Basketball Hall of Fame. The Rochester Royals were one of the best teams in the league at the time, although the Minneapolis Lakers, who had George Mikan, became the dominant team. Mikan would come in with the Lakers and everyone would say, "Look at the size of that guy." He was six feet, ten inches tall, so he'd hardly stand out on a court today, but back then Mikan was a giant. The Nationals played in a rickety old arena out on the Syracuse Fairgrounds against teams such as the Fort Wayne Pistons, Anderson Packers, Oshkosh

All-Stars, and Sheboygan Redskins. I did just the home games, and we didn't do re-creations on the road games. The Syracuse Nationals moved in 1963 and are now the Philadelphia 76ers.

For a couple of years I picked up some extra money by doing the public-address announcing at MacArthur Stadium for the Syracuse Chiefs, a farm club of the Cincinnati Reds in the International League. When the game ended, I'd return to the station and give a report of the game on my late sports show. I didn't have a car, but WSYR paid for a cab so I could get back to the station quickly after the game ended. I thought I was living pretty high in those days.

In 1948, while I was working in Syracuse, I had my first shot at college football announcing, although not for WSYR. I hooked up with the Atlantic Refining School of Broadcasters. In this case "school" meant not an educational institution but rather a stable of announcers assembled by the Atlantic Refining Company. I was assigned a game each week during the college football season. The Atlantic Refining Company conducted a seminar before each season. They brought all their announcers together in Philadelphia to talk about the upcoming season, rule changes, and so on. It was really nice.

Football, all things considered, is a relatively easy sport to announce because you have all week to prepare for a game. Later on when I was doing NFL games, I could watch the films from the previous games of each of the teams that would be playing in the game I'd be announcing. During the week I memorized the numbers of the players in the next game. After I was married, my wife helped me. When we were out for a drive, she would call out numbers and I'd try to identify the players.

I usually had a spotter in the booth with me, someone to point to the name of the player who had run the ball or made a tackle, but I usually had memorized the number so I didn't have to rely on the spotter. I was glad to have a spotter, though, once when the University of Richmond played at Boston College in the rain. Whenever it rained, I asked the coaches if the players might switch into a new jersey when their jersey became soaked. In those days, they didn't have extra jerseys with the same number, and I needed to know each players' second number. Before this game Ed Merrick, the Richmond coach, told me they didn't plan on changing uniforms, but the Richmond players got so wet and muddy that they switched jerseys after all. About half the players had new numbers, and I couldn't tell who some of them were. Fortunately, my spotter for that game was an injured Richmond player who was unable to play in that game, and he saved the day.

When I was assigned the Colgate-Bucknell game in Hamilton, New York, I arrived the night before the game, had a room at the Colgate Inn, and put together my spotting board of the numbers and names of the different players organized by their positions. I used India ink, which wouldn't run if it got wet. Back home in Syracuse, I couldn't find my bottle of India ink. The next year, I was assigned another Colgate game in Hamilton. I stayed in the same room at the Colgate Inn and there was my bottle of India ink, still on the desk.

After working in Syracuse for five years, I heard about an opening for a baseball announcer in Springfield, Massachusetts. The Springfield Cubs were replacing the Newark Bears, a Yankee farm club, in the International League, a Triple-A minor league. The Cubs would start play in the 1950 season, and their sponsor, the Hampden Brewing Company, held auditions for an announcer. Each applicant had to announce a game from a script with some details. It was like doing a re-creation from a Western Union ticker, and I lucked out and was hired. I had a broadcast partner, Dan Healey, who lived in Pittsfield, Massachusetts, about 50 miles from Pynchon Park, the Cubs' home in Springfield. We announced only the home games at the time. When the Cubs were on the road, we'd do re-creations in the studio.

Most announcers who did re-creations used sound effects for crowd noise and the crack of a bat hitting the ball. I never used sound effects. People knew I wasn't at the ball park. Why try to kid them? Besides, you need a good engineer to work the sound effects. If they're not done right, they sound awful. Instead, I liked having the noise of the Western Union ticker in the background. Someone would rip the paper out of the machine and hand it to me. It didn't contain a lot of details. If Ransom Jackson, the Cubs' third baseman, was batting and took a ball, the ticker would just say, "Ball one." I'd improvise and say it was inside, outside, high, or low. Once during a game at Buffalo the Western Union operator sent the message that Jack Wallaesa of the Cubs had hit a home run over the left-field fence. Then, a couple batters later, the operator sent a correction: Wallaesa's drive had not gone over the fence but had been caught by the left fielder. Since I had just announced it as a home run, I told the radio audience that I had made a mistake. I said I thought the umpire had signaled a home run for Wallaesa but he'd actually ruled that the left fielder had made a legal catch. I learned to let my announcing lag about a half inning behind the action.

My first broadcasts for the Cubs were from spring training in Florida. Dan Healey and I recorded interviews and reports on how the team was doing. The Springfield team trained in Haines City, which is close to the Baseball City complex where the Kansas City Royals now train, at the junction of Interstate 4 and U.S. Highway 27. The Cubs' stadium was a few miles south of Highway 27 in a rather swampy area. One day Ben Taylor, a young prospect trying

27

to make the team, was running in the outfield and stumbled over an alligator. That's the fastest I've ever seen anyone run off the field.

Haines City wasn't a lively town. The one movie theater was open only on Wednesday, Fridays, and Saturdays. About the only place to stay was the Polk Hotel. When I arrived for the first time in the spring of 1950, Stan Hack, the Cubs' manager, invited me to a party in his room. Stan's bathtub was full of ice with about three dozen bottles of beer. Stan Hack loved his beer and his cigars. A little later in the spring he invited me to a dinner at the Chalet Suzanne in Lake Wales, not far from Haines City, and also Joe Kuhel, who had had a long career with the Chicago White Sox and Washington Senators and now was managing the Kansas City Blues of the American Association. I thought, "Boy, this is great—a greenhorn announcer like me going out to dinner with Stan Hack and Joe Kuhel." We had a very nice dinner, and Stan and Joe swapped stories, which is one of the real charms of baseball.

The Cubs had some pretty good players at Springfield in 1950. Handsome Ransom Jackson, a third baseman, went on to have a few fine seasons with the Chicago Cubs. Bob Thurman, an outfielder, played for the Cincinnati Reds. Another outfielder, Carmen Mauro, was in between stints in the majors. Catcher Smoky Burgess and pitcher Warren Hacker went on to long careers in the majors.

On the way to Florida that first season in 1950 I stopped in Richmond, and while I was there, I met Katherine Meredith. Like me, Kathy had grown up in Richmond, but we had never met before. Now Kathy lived in Atlanta with her mother and stepfather, but she often stayed with her aunt in Richmond. We found we had a lot in common, including the fact that both our mothers were hatmakers. Kathy's mother made hats for movie stars, and Greer Garson wore one of her hats in a movie. Kathy and I were married on September 12 of that year, right after the Cubs' season ended. When I started broadcasting games in the majors, where the season extends longer that in the minors, I was never free on our anniversary. Years later, when I was with the Twins, someone asked what we did on our anniversary. I said, "Every other year, when the Twins are at home on September 12, Kathy has a real treat. She gets to go to a ball game."

Kathy went with me to spring training in 1951. A shortstop named Jack Wallaesa had purchased a new Pontiac during spring training, but Big Bill Kelly, the new manager, refused to give him permission to drive home, so Jack asked Kathy and me if we would drive his car back to Springfield, rather than take the train. In Georgia we drove through torrential rain on the highway, which was built up on dikes, and there were frogs all over the road. Trying to dodge the frogs and keep from driving off the dike was scaring me out of my wits. And we had to keep on going through the dark and rain because we couldn't find a motel with a vacancy. It was a long way between towns. We'd finally see the lights of a motel ahead, only to be told when we got there, "Sorry, no vacancy."

Things didn't go well for the Springfield Cubs in the next few years. After a fifth-place finish in 1950, Springfield fell to last place for their next three years and then dropped out of the International League. In 1951 Stan Hack and some of the better players were transferred to the Los Angeles Angels, the Chicago Cubs' other Triple-A farm team.

The Chicago Cubs organization seemed to want its Springfield team to get off to a good start, so it initially was well stocked with players, but then the Angels received the top talent.

One of the new players in 1951 was Vern Morgan, who replaced Jackson at third. I later became reacquainted with

Vern when he became a coach for the Twins. He reminded me of an incident when they were being swept in a double-header in Springfield. They had already blown a big lead and lost the first game and were on the verge of blowing another in the nightcap. Then a close play went against the Cubs, and Bill Kelly started to charge out after the umpires, but when he jumped up, he hit his head on the top of the dugout and almost knocked himself out. As he slowly sank back on the dugout bench, the players couldn't help laughing. They quit laughing when Kelly made them stay after the doubleheader for a two-hour workout.

During the years I was in Springfield, I was still announcing college football for the Atlantic Refining Company and also had my first chance to announce hockey. Eddie Shore, the great defenseman for the Boston Bruins in the 1920s and 1930s, now owned the Springfield Indians in the American Hockey League. He had heard me announcing baseball for the Cubs and told Hampden Brewing Company he wanted me to announce their games. The folks at Hampden thought I'd be tickled pink at the offer, but I said, "I can't do hockey. I don't know anything about hockey. I grew up in the South, and there was no hockey."

"I don't care if he hasn't done it before," Eddie Shore told the sponsor. "Tell him to come over here, and I'll teach him how to do it." Eddie Shore had been one of the roughest and meanest men ever to play hockey, but he was very patient with me as he taught me how to announce the game.

When the minor-league baseball season finished in 1953, Kathy and I visited her family in Atlanta. There, I auditioned for an announcing job with the Atlanta Crackers, a minor-league baseball team in the Southern League. Jim Woods, who had been doing the games, was leaving to do play-by-play for the New York Yankees. The Crackers hadn't made a decision by the time we left. When Kathy and

I got back to Springfield, I was told that somebody from Philadelphia had been trying to reach me. It was Bill Givens, whom I had worked with in Syracuse, and he told me that KYW in Philadelphia was looking for a sports announcer to do four different sports shows on radio and one on television, in addition to Princeton football. I landed the job.

I started doing the Princeton games almost immediately. Charlie Caldwell was their coach, and they had a very good team. Princeton, New Jersey, is about 50 miles north of Philadelphia. For the home games we'd drive up on Friday and stay at the Princeton Inn. On Friday night they'd have a dinner for the press on with one of the coaches on hand to preview the game for us.

At the time the Ivy League football conference was still tough, and there was a great college-football atmosphere, especially with all those great rivalries such as Yale and Harvard. I saw pre-game tailgating at Princeton for the first time. And for the first time I traveled with a team. Instead of doing re-creations for their road games, I'd travel with Princeton to places like Harvard in Cambridge, Massachusetts, and Dartmouth in New Hampshire.

The whole game of football was different back then. Most teams played a single-wing offense, with a quarterback, fullback, wingback, and tailback. The quarterback was a blocking back, and the tailback took the snap from center and did most of the passing. In this one-platoon football, players stayed on the field for both offense and defense. Now it's highly specialized, but back then a guy had to be able to do all sorts of things.

After announcing Princeton football for a couple of years, I became the regular football announcer for Temple in Philadelphia. Rutgers, Villanova, Bucknell, and Lehigh were some of the outstanding teams in the conference with Temple.

I didn't expect to announce baseball even though Philadelphia had two major-league teams: the Athletics in the American League and the Phillies in the National League. The games of both teams were carried by other stations, WIBG for the Athletics and WFIL for the Phillies. But in early 1954 I got a call from Les Quailey of N. W. Ayer Advertising, one of the big sponsors for both the Phillies and the A's. He said they were planning to expand their television coverage of baseball and would need another announcer for radio broadcasts at home. He asked if I would be interested in being the swing man, announcing about a hundred home games with the Phillies and Athletics. He said that since I wouldn't have to travel, I could still do most of my sports shows on KYW. I definitely wanted to do it, but I wasn't sure my boss at KYW would take kindly to my announcing on other stations. As it turned out, though, he told me to go ahead and do it. He figured my exposure in announcing the A's and Phillies would increase my ratings with KYW.

Both teams shared the same stadium, Shibe Park, which was later renamed Connie Mack Stadium. It was a good old baseball park—a lot of character on the inside and stately architecture on the outside. There wasn't much in the way of parking. Most of the fans took public transportation. Those of us in the media arrived early enough to find a spot on the street, but, as with Griffith Stadium in Washington, it was smart to pay a kid 50 cents to keep an eye on your car.

Although I didn't travel at all, I saw all the major-league teams that came through Shibe Park. It was at this time that I first met Harmon Killebrew. He was with the Senators, primarily sitting on the bench and occasionally getting into a game as a pinch runner. He was a "bonus baby," having signed a $30,000 contract with the Senators in 1954. By a peculiar rule of that time, if a team signed a player for more than a certain bonus—$30,000 was well over the limit—the team couldn't send the player to the minors for at least two years. I never understood the rule. Killebrew spent two years doing virtually nothing when he could have been developing his skills in the minors. The Senators had to wait until 1956 to send him down for seasoning, and in 1959 he became a regular in the Washington lineup. Had he been able to go to the minors immediately, he probably would have been playing regularly two years earlier and would have finished his career with more than 600 home runs.

It was amazing he hit so many home runs with the Senators, considering the distance from home plate to left field at Griffith Stadium: 405 feet down the line, the longest dimension of any park in the majors. I asked Harmon if he had known how deep it was when he signed. He said he never gave any thought to it. He was so strong, though, that he could reach the fence in any park. He hit 42 home runs for Washington in 1959. Two years later, the Senators moved to Minnesota. With the much friendlier dimensions of Metropolitan Stadium, Harmon hit 40 or more home runs another seven times. Only Babe Ruth had more seasons of 40 or more home runs. Harmon had very large arms. I asked if he did a lot of exercising in the off-season, and he said, "No, I just swing the bat."

The A's didn't have much of a team in 1954. Connie Mack had retired as manager five years before. Eddie Joost was now the manager, and he didn't have much in the way of players. Gus Zernial, who had hit 42 homers the year before, had some problems in 1954 and dropped to 14 home runs. Vic Power, who later became a slick-fielding first baseman with the Twins, was a starting outfielder for the A's that year. The Athletics finished last in the American League, with a record of 51-103. The A's drew barely 300,000 people to their games that year.

The Phillies floundered a bit in 1954 but still finished in fourth place. Just four years earlier the Phillies had won the National League pennant with their "Whiz Kids," and a lot of those Whiz Kids were still with the team. Second baseman Granny Hamner hit .299 with 13 home runs and 89 RBIs. Third baseman Willie "Puddin' Head" Jones hit .271 with 12 homers. In the outfield Del Ennis had an outstanding season with 25 home runs and 119 runs batted in, and Richie Ashburn, their great leadoff man, had a batting average of .313. Ashburn was elected to the Hall of Fame in 1995. It was an honor long overdue.

Robin Roberts led the National League with 23 wins, 337 innings pitched (about 100 more than most starting pitchers would throw today), and 185 strikeouts. Robin first won 20 games for the Phillies during their pennant-winning season of 1950 and continued to win at least 20 through 1955. He also led the league in wins from 1952 to 1955 and in innings pitched for five straight years starting in 1951. Despite all the innings he pitched, he walked only 50 to 60 batters a year. Yet Roberts didn't seem to have outstanding stuff. He was mainly a two-pitch pitcher: fastball and curve. His curveball didn't have much of a break on it, either. Somebody once said to him, "I knew you had a pretty good fastball, but I didn't know you threw a slider."

"Slider?" Roberts said. "That was my curveball." Like Bert Blyleven some years later, Roberts gave up a lot of home runs but usually with the bases empty. What made Roberts outstanding was his great control. He could put that ball just about anywhere he wanted to. Robin was quite a nice man, too. With him on Saturday mornings I did a radio show with baseball questions for kids to answer and win prizes.

It was a lot of fun doing the Phillies and Athletics in 1954, but it came to an end after one season because the A's moved to Kansas City. They had fallen to the bottom of the well and couldn't climb out. Nobody came to their games, and they decided to try playing somewhere else.

In the 1950s teams started moving to adjust to the shifting demographics, and the first teams to go were from the cities with more than one team—Chicago, Boston, St. Louis, Philadelphia, and New York. In 1953 the Boston Braves moved to Milwaukee. The next year the St. Louis Browns went to Baltimore. A few years later both National League teams in New York moved out to the West Coast. When Philadelphia lost the Athletics to Kansas City, my job as the swing announcer was eliminated because all of a sudden the city had more baseball announcers than it could use. Byrum Saam and Claude Herring had been with the A's, and Gene Kelly and George Walsh with the Phillies. Now George Walsh returned to Louisville, where he had worked before, and the other three announcers went with the Phillies.

I still had a good sports job with KYW, but I was hooked on announcing baseball.

Ernie Harwell was my mentor when we both announced
for the Baltimore Orioles. We continued to see a lot of each
other through the years.

For the Birds

I stayed in Philadelphia through 1956, but I was getting tired of studio stuff. I wanted to go out, see more, and do play-by-play on baseball again.

Then the National Brewing Company, which had owned the rights to Oriole games, switched to the Washington Senators, and since the sponsors hired the announcers, there was a shake-up in the broadcast booth. Ernie Harwell, who had been with the Orioles since they moved to Baltimore in 1954, stayed with the Orioles, but Chuck Thompson went to Washington with the National Brewing Company, leaving an opening in Baltimore. I sent an application and an audition tape to the new sponsor for Orioles, Gunther Brewing Company. They interviewed me in mid-November, gave me the third degree, and said they'd be in touch. On Christmas morning the Gunther Brewing Company's ad agency phoned me with an offer for the Orioles' announcing job.

Nowadays the announcer is usually employed by the radio or television station, but in those days the sponsors, which were usually breweries, really called the shots. One or two sponsors bought the broadcast rights to an entire game, and although they usually sold off some of the commercial spots, they would often be sole sponsor for large segments of a game—say, three innings at a time. Since they held the rights to the games, they had the biggest say in choosing the announcers. The team and the radio station might have the right to approve the announcers, but unless they felt there was something drastically wrong with someone, they'd go along with the sponsor's choice. Chuck Thompson, whom I replaced in Baltimore, started his career in Reading, Pennsylvania, and then came to Philadelphia. In 1950 he went to Baltimore with the understanding that when Baltimore got a major-league franchise, he'd be the announcer because National Brewing Company would acquire the rights. Then after three years with Baltimore, when National Brewing switched to the Senators, Thompson went with them. He spent his entire career with National Brewing Company and later came back to Baltimore as a result.

Ernie Harwell, on the other hand, stayed with the Orioles despite the change in sponsors. Ernie learned that the Orioles would be having a different sponsor in a news release that Ernie read between innings of one of the Orioles' games. He told me it was pretty difficult to keep his concentration for the rest of the game. Ernie had started as an announcer in the majors with the Brooklyn Dodgers in 1948. A couple of years later he was with the Giants, and he was the television announcer in 1951 when Bobby Thomson hit his home run to win the pennant for the Giants. Ernie joined the Orioles broadcast crew in 1954, when the team moved to Baltimore from St. Louis. He eventually moved on to Detroit, where he became one of the best-known announcers in baseball, and in 1981 he was elected to the broadcasting wing of the Baseball Hall of Fame, the first announcer to receive this honor while still active.

How Ernie got to the majors is a story in itself. He was doing the play-by-play for the Atlanta Crackers of the Southern League in 1948, when Branch Rickey of the Brooklyn Dodgers called Earl Mann, the owner of the Atlanta Crackers, and asked for a favor. Red Barber, the Dodgers' regular announcer, had taken ill, and Rickey wanted Mann to release Harwell from his contract so he could announce the Dodger games. This put Mann on the spot. He couldn't easily replace Ernie in midseason, but he didn't want to stand in the way of Ernie's chance to announce in the majors. Since the Crackers were weak in the catching department, Mann told Rickey he would trade Ernie for a catcher. Rickey sent the Crackers Cliff Dapper from the Dodgers' farm team in St. Paul, and that's how Ernie made it to the big leagues.

Ernie's not only a great announcer but also a song writer, and he's written on many subjects and even patented a couple of inventions. When he took me under his wing in 1957, I learned a lot about baseball and other aspects of life. In Cleveland, on my first road trip with a baseball club, a night game was scheduled, but it rained all afternoon. At 4:30 Ernie phoned to tell me the game had been postponed, but at 5:00 he took me out to the stadium anyway for the pregame meal in the press room. "No sense letting all that good food go to waste," he said.

Most of the teams traveled by airplane, but the Orioles' manager, Paul Richards, preferred trains, like Halsey Hall, my broadcast partner a few years later. Imagine what modern-day players would say about that, but back then the manager called the shots. Once we finished a road trip in Kansas City on Sunday and had a home game scheduled for Tuesday night. Our train left Kansas City at 11:00 on Sunday night, arrived in Chicago at 8:00 the next morning, and departed for Baltimore at 4:00 in the afternoon. We didn't get home until Tuesday morning. I didn't mind the long hours traveling, though. The team had a private diner on the train, and traveling like this helped me get to know the players better. The Orioles stuck with train travel until 1961, when the American League added a team in Los Angeles. We couldn't avoid flying anymore.

Paul Richards also called the shots for spring training. He was from Waxahachie, Texas, and really liked the Southwest, so the Orioles trained in Scottsdale, Arizona, along with a few other teams. Over Richards' objections, the Orioles' owner eventually moved their training facilities to Miami, so fans could more conveniently travel to spring training games.

At spring training in 1957 one of the writers, Lou Hatter, liked to kid Ernie Harwell and me about how easy we had it. All we had to do was broadcast a game, he said, while he had to cover the game and scrounge around for a side story. So Ernie invited him to the broadcast booth to announce a game for a couple of innings. Lou accepted the challenge and was having a pretty good time doing the play-by-play until Billy Gardner, the Orioles' second baseman, came to bat and was hit in the back with a pitched ball. As usual, Billy had a big wad of tobacco in his cheek, and the jolt caused him to swallow his chaw. As Gardner lay wretching on the ground, Hatter was overwhelmed trying to describe what was happening. "Here, you take the mike," he said to Ernie, and he left the booth.

Gardner later played for and then managed the Twins. Lenny Green was another future Twin who played for the Orioles while I was there, and Kathy and I got to know him pretty well. The regular third baseman for Baltimore was George Kell, who had had many great seasons with the Detroit Tigers. After that year, 1957, Kell retired with a lifetime batting average of .306. He was elected to the Hall of Fame in 1983. He became a broadcaster for the Tigers and worked as Ernie Harwell's partner for a long time in Detroit.

As one Hall of Fame third baseman was wrapping up his career with Baltimore in 1957, another was just starting. Brooks Robinson had been up briefly with the Orioles each of the previous two seasons. He played in 50 games in 1957 and, after Kell retired, became a fixture at third base. Even in 1957, when I first watched Brooks play, you could tell he was a natural-born third baseman with quick reflexes. He didn't have the strongest arm I'd ever seen on a third baseman, but it was an accurate arm. During his 23 seasons in the majors, all for Baltimore, he became one of the greatest third basemen in the history of the game. He was voted the American League Most Valuable Player in 1964 and was elected to the Baseball Hall of Fame in 1983, along with George Kell, the man he had succeeded at third base for the Orioles.

The Orioles finished in fifth place in 1957 with a 76-76 record, their best showing since they'd moved to Baltimore. Previously they had been the St. Louis Browns, one of the worst teams in the American League. Now they were making progress.

While announcing Oriole games in 1957 I kept track of pitches, as I had learned from Gene Kelly in Philadelphia two years before. I had noticed that Gene made a mark in his scorebook after each pitch. Between innings I asked him about it. He said, "I'm counting pitches. At the top of the box for each player, I put a slash for each pitch—on the left if it's a ball, on the right if it's a strike." I adopted that method in Baltimore so I could always announce how many pitches a pitcher had thrown. For a relief pitcher, who goes only a few innings at a time, that number doesn't mean much, but it's useful information with the starting pitcher. After all, in determining if he might be tiring out, what matters is not how many innings he's gone but how many pitches he's thrown. If a starter has only 80 pitches through seven innings, you can figure he's in pretty good shape, but if he's thrown 100 pitches by the fourth inning, you know he won't be around much longer, and that's worth mentioning to the radio audience.

Baltimore hosted the All-Star Game in 1958. It was a pretty good game, with the American League winning, 4-3. The Orioles had a couple of players in the game. Gus Triandos was the starting catcher, and Billy O'Dell pitched the final three innings of the game, protecting the American League lead by retiring all nine batters in just 27 pitches.

Billy O'Dell, a native of South Carolina, was a very nice young man. His nickname was Digger. One night he was pitching against the Yankees, who had Zack Monroe on the mound. I had just bought my wife a beautiful Persian kitten, which we had yet to name. We decided we'd name it after the winning pitcher in the game that night. The Yankees won, so we had a cat named Zack. Of course, had the Orioles won, we would have had a cat named Digger.

Catcher Gus Triandos had good power, hitting 30 home runs in 1958, but was very slow of foot. One winter Paul Richards sent him down to the Naval Academy in Annapolis to have the track coach work with him to increase his speed. The next spring Richards asked if the coach had been able to help him. "He sure did," Gus replied. "Now instead of always getting thrown out by five steps at first base, it'll be only three."

Triandos was an outstanding fielder and twice led American League catchers in assists—and twice in passed balls, too, primarily because of a new pitcher the Orioles acquired in August 1958. Hoyt Wilhelm, who had pitched for the Minneapolis Millers in 1950 and 1951, came to Baltimore on waivers after being released by Cleveland. He was the greatest knuckleballer ever. The only people who hate knuckleballers more than batters are the catchers who have to catch them. Once, with Wilhelm on the mound, catcher Joe Ginsberg had three passed balls in one inning. Shortly after that, Paul Richards, himself a former catcher, and

Harry Brecheen, the Orioles' pitching coach, developed an oversize mitt for catching knuckleballs.

In a game against the Yankees in Baltimore, on September 20, less than a month after joining the Orioles, Wilhelm pitched a no-hitter, winning, 1-0, on a home run by Triandos. In the ninth inning Hank Bauer of the Yankees led off by trying to bunt for a hit. He was thrown out, but that didn't sit well with the Orioles: there's an unwritten rule against bunting to break up no-hitter. Of course, with the Yankees down by only a run, Bauer was just trying to get on base with the tying run. Wilhelm completed that no-hitter with only about 85 pitches. After the game Paul Richards said it was too bad they weren't playing a double-header. He would have started Wilhelm in the second game, too.

Although the Indians had given up on Wilhelm by releasing him in 1958, he went on to a Hall of Fame career as a reliever and became the only pitcher to appear in more than 1,000 games. In 1959, starting more games than at any other time in his career, he won his first nine decisions and at one point had an earned-run average under a run per game. The batters had plenty of trouble with Wilhelm that year, but one night in Chicago a swarm of gnats nearly did him in. Hoyt was on the mound when he was attacked by huge clouds of gnats. Finally, the White Sox drove the gnats away with fireworks that were intended for a post-game display.

In 1952, when Wilhelm came up with the New York Giants, he hit a home run in his first at-bat in the major leagues, although it was the only home he ever hit in the majors. For the next few years, the Orioles had quite a few good-hitting pitchers such as Milt Pappas, Chuck Estrada, Jerry Walker, Jack Fisher, and Steve Barber. None of them however, could compare with Jack Harshman.

Harshman had started his career as a first baseman and had been a big slugger for the Minneapolis Millers of the

American Association about ten years before. When he eventually switched to pitching, he remained a dangerous hitter. In 1958 he hit eight home runs, including two in one game.

As a left-handed pitcher, Harshman was especially effective in night games at Memorial Stadium in Baltimore, because he was pitching out of the scoreboard lights in right-center field. That is, his motion was such that the scoreboard was behind his release point of the ball, and a batter trying to pick the ball up out of his hand was looking right into the scoreboard lights. Jack was a good guy. We used to call him Apple Jack because he liked a nip now and then. He had some back troubles and wore a corset. Once in spring training in Arizona he put it on and almost jumped through the ceiling. There was a scorpion in the corset. When Jack pulled the corset tight, the scorpion stung him.

In those days some games had to have curfews, especially the final game of a series when one or both teams had to catch planes or trains. Curfews are much rarer these days, and even when they do occur the rules allow for an inning to be completed. Today a game stopped by a curfew is considered suspended, to be resumed at a later date. In the 1950s one game between the Orioles and White Sox at Memorial Stadium had a 10:20 p.m. curfew to allow the White Sox enough time to catch a flight out of the Baltimore airport. Chicago held a 4-3 lead with two out in the bottom of ninth, and the curfew time was approaching. White Sox manager Al Lopez went to the mound, presumably to stall a little. When the conference was over, it was 10:19. Dick Williams of the Orioles was stepping into the batter's box to face Paul LePalme. All LePalme had to do was throw a couple pitches in the dirt, and the game would end on account of the curfew. Instead, he laid one right over the plate, and Williams hit it out of the park for a home run. The game finished as a tie and had to be replayed in its entirety. The Orioles won the makeup game.

A few years later I witnessed something more bizarre during a game against the Athletics at Kansas City. There were few fans there, but many of them didn't agree with plate umpire Bob Stewart's calls and were giving him a pretty hard time most of the game. Then in the top of the ninth inning Stewart made a controversial call in favor of the Orioles, and six Baltimore runs followed. One fan climbed over the railing on the first-base side and walked toward home plate. Stewart saw him coming, took off his mask, and told him to get out. But the guy kept going and pounded Stewart one right on the jaw. He also decked an usher who had followed him out there. A couple of the umpires, Ed Hurley from third base and Hank Soar from first, rushed over, but they couldn't hold the incensed fan, a very strong steel worker. He grabbed Soar's arm and flipped him, although Soar had been a professional football player and was not little. Finally some cops ran out and subdued the guy. A couple of days later Charlie Finley, the Athletics' owner, announced that he was giving this guy a season pass for his loyalty to Kansas City. I'm not sure that's loyalty. In most places the guy would have been banned from the ballpark.

Another event—this one falling more into the memorable than strange category even though it involved heroics against, not for, the Orioles—happened in 1959. In a night game at Baltimore in June of that year Rocky Colavito of the Cleveland Indians hit four home runs. Each homer was farther than the previous one.

Although they had a rough time with Colavito that night, the Orioles were assembling a pretty decent pitching staff at the time. Twenty-year-old Milt Pappas won 15 games for the Orioles in 1959, and Jerry Walker, only three months older, had an 11-10 record. Jack Fisher, born a month after Walker,

45

struggled in relief, winning just one game, but that one win was really something. On September 11, 1959, in the first game of a double-header against the White Sox, in one of his rare starts that year, Jack retired the first 19 batters before Nellie Fox broke up his perfect game with a hit with one out in the seventh inning. Jack finished with a shutout. In the second game Baltimore and Chicago battled through 15 scoreless innings before the Orioles finally won it, 1-0, on a run-scoring single by Brooks Robinson in the last of the 16th. Jerry Walker had pitched the entire game for the Orioles. He threw something like 175 pitches in that 16-inning shutout.

Even with the good young arms on the staff, the Orioles dropped to sixth place with a 74-80 record in 1959. The next season, though, they were joined by a couple more young pitchers and really took off, finding themselves in a great pennant race with the Yankees into September. Chuck Estrada, who turned 22 before the 1960 season started, won 18 games in his rookie season with Baltimore. Another rookie, Steve Barber, who was 21, had a 10-7 record. With Estrada, Barber, Walker, Pappas, and Fisher no more than 22 years old, the Orioles' pitching staff became known as the Kiddie Korps. All except Barber were right-handed and so benefited from a quirk at Memorial Stadium. Behind the center-field fence was a white house, and when a right-handed pitcher released the ball, that white house was in the background of the batter's sight line, making the ball difficult to see, as with those scoreboard lights that helped Jack Harshman. Eventually the team put up some foliage between the center-field fence and the house, providing a better batter's eye. But the Oriole hurlers were just plain good in 1960. For the first time Baltimore had pennant fever.

The Orioles got off to a slow start in April but improved in May and briefly held first place. They had a tough time right before the All-Star break, losing 11 of 15, but then they hit a hot stretch in early August and moved into a tie for first place. They were quickly knocked from the top spot, getting swept in a two-game series by the Yankees, who then went on a hot streak of their own. The Yankees couldn't shake the Orioles, though, and held only a one-game lead on September 2, when the two teams started a three-game weekend series at Memorial Stadium.

The Kiddie Korps came through. Milt Pappas tossed a three-hit shutout in the opener, and the Orioles won, 5-0, moving into a tie for first. In the Saturday game Jack Fisher hurled another shutout, his second-straight shutout, giving the Orioles a 2-0 win and first place all to themselves. In the last game of the series Chuck Estrada took a no-hitter into the seventh inning. Then Moose Skowron singled with two out, and the Yankees finally scratched out a couple of runs. But Hoyt Wilhelm relieved Estrada, and the Orioles won, 6-2, to finish the sweep.

Baltimore now had a two-game lead, but 20 of its last 22 games would be on the road. On the following Thursday night in Cleveland, Jack Fisher hurled his third consecutive shutout. The game was scoreless until the seventh inning, when the Orioles exploded against Cleveland starter Dick Stigman. They scored nine runs in that inning and won the game, 9-0. A week later, tied with the Yankees again, the Orioles moved into Yankee Stadium for a four-game series. Barney Kremenko, a veteran New York writer, said before the first game, "If either team sweeps, the race is over. But, of course, that won't happen."

But the Yankees won all four games. In the last one Ralph Terry even held the Orioles hitless until the eighth inning. The sweep was the start of a 15-game winning streak for the Yankees, who won the American League flag by eight games. Still, the Orioles came in second, and the Baltimore fans were pretty excited about their team.

As the Orioles finished that season, there was a memorable series with the Red Sox. Ted Williams, who had come up with Boston in 1939 and had become one of baseball's greatest hitters, was retiring. The Red Sox still had another series on the road, but Williams had announced that he would not accompany them. These games with the Orioles at Fenway Park in Boston would be his last.

It was a pretty emotional time for everyone when he came to bat for the last time in the final game of that series. On the air I said, "It wouldn't surprise me if he hits one out of here." The next thing I knew, Williams sent a pitch sailing into the right-field seats. He had done it—a home run in his last trip to the plate in the major leagues. As he circled the bases, everyone wondered if he'd finally tip his hat to the fans. He didn't. In the next inning the Red Sox manager, Mike Higgins, took Williams out of the game, but first he sent him out to his position in left field. Then when Carroll Hardy relieved him, Ted got one last ovation as he ran back to the dugout. He still didn't tip his hat.

A footnote. My wife, Kathy, taped many of my broadcasts so my mother could listen to them, but she didn't happen to tape this game. When she heard that I had more or less predicted Williams' homer in his last at-bat, she tried to find someone who had taped the broadcast. Unfortunately no one, not even the radio station, had.

I had a new broadcast partner in 1960. Ernie Harwell went to Detroit to become an announcer for the Tigers, and Bob Murphy, who had been with the Boston Red Sox since 1954, joined me. A couple years later, Murphy became part of the broadcast team for the New York Mets and has been there ever since. His brother was Jack Murphy, a sportswriter in San Diego, and the San Diego Padres' stadium is now Jack Murphy Stadium. Bob Murphy was a good guy to work with. Whenever he made a mistake, he'd say, "That's why they put erasers on pencils."

The American League expanded in 1961, with new teams in Los Angeles and Washington, D.C., and the league finally allowed Calvin Griffith to move his Washington Senators to Minnesota to become the Twins, while one of the new teams, also called the Senators, was placed in the nation's capital. When the Orioles played the Twins in Minnesota, we stayed at the St. Paul Hotel in downtown St. Paul. Even though Metropolitan Stadium, home of the Twins, was in suburban Bloomington, the Twins were perceived as more closely associated with Minneapolis than St. Paul. I think the Twins wanted some of the visiting teams to stay in St. Paul to make that city feel more involved.

There were some interesting games played between the Twins and Orioles in Minnesota that year. In August the Orioles swept a three-game series at Met Stadium. In the last game Milt Pappas not only hurled a two-hit shutout but also hit two home runs.

Another big moment came in early May in the first game the Orioles played in Minnesota. Jim Gentile hit grand slams his first two times up, in the first and second innings, and finished with nine RBIs in the game. Just two years before Jim had played the entire year with the St. Paul Saints of the American Association. He possessed great power and was a very good fielder at first base, but he was also his own worst enemy. When things went wrong, his annoyance would affect his performance. But Jim had a great season in 1961, ending up with 46 home runs and 141 runs batted in. He had been tied for the league lead in RBIs, but when Roger Maris of the Yankees hit his 61st home run in the last game of the season, he got the RBI he needed to finish ahead of Gentile. (As it turns out, it could be that Maris and Gentile ended up tied for the league lead in RBIs. In 1995, a member of the Society for American Baseball Research discovered that, because of a record-keeping error by an official scorer, Maris was credited with one too many RBIs in 1961. As a result, the official records may be changed and Gentile listed as the American League's RBI co-leader in 1961.)

I saw Maris' 60th home run, which tied Babe Ruth's single-season record, since Maris hit it off Jack Fisher in a game against the Orioles. There was, however, a controversy about whether Maris had really tied the record. When Ruth hit his 60 home runs, in 1927, the season was 154 games long. In 1961, with the addition of two teams, the season was expanded to 162 games. Many people, including Baseball Commissioner Ford Frick, didn't want to see the Babe's record broken if it took more games to do it. They said that a new home-run record would have to be set within 154 games. Maris was past that number when he hit his 60th and 61st. In the early 1990s it was finally ruled that Roger Maris was the record holder. By that time Roger was dead. The controversy and the pressure as he approached Ruth's total took a toll on Maris, to the point that his hair began falling out in big clumps. I talked to him the day after he hit number 60. He was very tense. He later said that baseball quit being fun for him after he broke the record. Since the Orioles had one more game left in their series against the Yankees, we thought we might see Maris hit number 61 and pass the Babe's mark, but he didn't play in that game. He said he was just "plain bushed" and needed the rest, especially with the World Series coming up, since the Yankees had already clinched the pennant. With only a few games left in the regular season you might have expected him to take every opportunity to hit another home run, but Roger placed a higher priority on helping his team in the World Series.

With about a month left in the 1961 season Paul Richards resigned as manager and was replaced by Lum Harris. Richards was about to become the general manager of the Houston Colt 45s, now the Houston Astros, a new team scheduled to start play in the National League in 1962. Richards had been the Orioles' only manager during my years in Baltimore. He was a fine manager and quite a character. Once before a night game in Kansas City he invited me for a steak dinner at the Golden Ox. Afterward, as we left the restaurant to get a cab, he was deep in thought. He walked over to a car, opened the back door, and hopped in. The only problem was that this wasn't a cab—it was a police car.

When he first came to Baltimore in 1955, he was the Orioles' field manager and also their general manager. For the first couple of years he had carte blanche for spending the team's money, but in 1957, my first year announcing their games, the Oriole stockholders hired Bill Walsingham to establish a more responsible budget. Richards, however, still enjoyed taking media people out to dinner. One Saturday in Detroit he invited everyone up to his suite at the Sheraton Cadillac to watch either the Kentucky Derby or one of the other Triple Crown races. After the race he asked, "Who wants to go out to eat?" About 14 of us accepted his offer. He took us to a restaurant called Mario's, where he knew the staff very well. When you were there with Paul Richards, you didn't bother to order; he just had them bring out all sorts of food and drinks. We ran up a pretty good tab. As we were finishing eating, Paul looked at his watch and said, "Hey, I've got to get to the ballpark." He slapped Walsingham on the shoulder and said, "Bill, take care of this, will you?" And he walked out. So much for getting the team back on any kind of financial track.

A few other things stood out about the 1961 season with the Orioles. One was the pitching of southpaw Steve Barber.

In his second season in the majors, Barber not only won 18 games but also led the American League with eight shutouts. He had a sinking-type fastball and what they called a heavy ball. You don't hear that expression anymore, but when a batter hit a "heavy ball" it felt like he was hitting a brick. Estrada was a bigger strikeout pitcher, but Barber could get the batters to hit a lot of grounders with that heavy ball of his. Although he had control problems in his first few years with the Orioles, Barber won 20 games in 1963 and struck out nearly twice as many batters as he walked. Then he started having arm problems and was never again as effective as in those outstanding early seasons.

He reminded me of Steve Dalkowski, another left-hander in the minor leagues of the Oriole organization. In 1957, at the age of 18 in his first season of pro ball, Dalkowski struck out 121 batters in 62 innings, nearly two an inning. In the next year he pitched for three teams at different levels of the minors and had 232 strikeouts in 118 innings. These were phenomenal totals. But he was walking more batters than he struck out. He was with us in spring training for a couple of years. Watching him pitch on the sidelines, I could hear that ball hum when he threw it. He didn't seem to be all that wild on the sidelines, but as soon as he got into a game, he just couldn't throw strikes. Once, during a spring-training game against the Indians, Richards brought Dalkowski in to pitch the ninth. His first two pitches sailed to the backstop. The batter moved to the far corner of the batter's box, as far from the plate as he could get. On another occasion during spring training, when Connie Johnson, one of our pitchers, wanted to take some extra batting practice, Dalkowski was sent out to pitch for him. Connie went to the dugout and came back to the batter's box wearing a catcher's mask, chest protector, and shin guards. Dalkowski pitched nine seasons in the minors and never made it to the major

leagues because of his lack of control. He put so many runners on base with walks that he lost nearly twice as many
games as he won during his professional career. Fortunately
he never killed anyone.

A veteran who contributed a lot to the Orioles in 1961 was
Dave Philley, a switch hitter. Even though he was 41, he set a
major-league record with 24 pinch hits that year. For most
players spring training was a time to get rid of the extra
weight they had put on over the winter. Philley was just the
opposite. He told me he liked to arrive at training camp
about four or five pounds underweight so he could then eat
whatever he wanted. It must have worked. That guy could
sure hit.

Another player who joined us that year was Marv
Throneberry, a gawky first baseman who had good power
when he connected, although it wasn't that often. The next
year the Orioles sent him to the New York Mets, an expansion team that lost 120 games. Throneberry was so inept
with them that he became a fan favorite. He epitomized
how bad the entire team was, and they called him Mar-
velous Marv. Like Steve Bilko or Rocky Nelson, Throneberry was a great hitter in the minor leagues, but he never
got over that last hurdle.

The Orioles had a great season in 1961, winning 95 games,
their most ever. But that year the Tigers won 101 and the
Yankees 109, so the Orioles finished third, 14 games out of
first place. They were a good young team, though, definitely
on their way up. Another change in sponsors was looming
for the Orioles, though, so I'd probably be out of a job. But I
heard about another up-and-coming team that might have
an opening for an announcer in 1962. It was in a place I had
been just a few times but already liked: Minnesota.

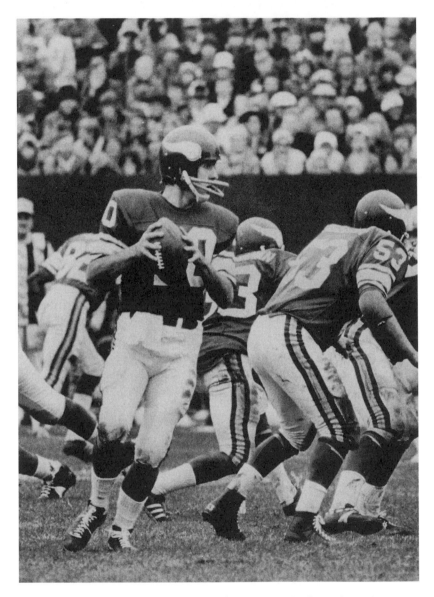

Fran Tarkenton provided a lot of excitement in the early years
of the Vikings. *WCCO Radio*.

Viking Log

I had already had a good taste of Minnesota before becoming the announcer for the Twins for the 1962 season, because in 1961 I was the regular announcer for another Minnesota team, the Vikings of the National Football League.

In the winter after the 1960 baseball season I received a call from Art Lund of Campbell-Mithun, the Minnesota advertising agency used by the Hamm Brewing Company, which had recently expanded to the East Coast and become a partial sponsor of the Orioles' games. Mr. Lund asked if I would be interested in announcing on network television for the Minnesota Vikings, the state's new expansion franchise, which would begin play in the National Football League in 1961. At that time the networks assigned announcers to the games of a particular team, whereas today an announcing crew covers a variety of teams. I said I was interested. Bill MacPhail, the sports director for CBS Television, then asked for an audition tape, and he soon offered me the job.

I hadn't done any football for a few years, not since moving to Baltimore, and since I was still involved with the Orioles' games in 1961, I had no any opportunity to see the Vikings during the preseason, in which they didn't win any of their exhibition games. That was to be expected for an expansion team. The Dallas Cowboys had been winless in their first season in the league the year before.

I certainly didn't expect the Vikings to go the entire year without a victory but it didn't look like they'd get a win in their season opener against the powerful Chicago Bears at Met Stadium. The Bears' head coach was the legendary George "Papa Bear" Halas, and the Vikings' coach was Norm Van Brocklin, who had taken this first coaching job after quarterbacking the Philadelphia Eagles to the NFL title just a few months before. The Vikings had some experience in their backfield with a couple of players they had taken in the expansion draft: Hugh McElhenny from the San Francisco 49ers and Mel Triplett from the New York Giants. They were both pretty well along in their careers. Probably their best pick in the expansion draft was offensive lineman Grady Alderman from Detroit.

In that first game George Shaw started at quarterback for the Vikings and led a first-quarter drive that resulted in a Mike Mercer field goal for a 3-0 lead. Late in the first quarter Shaw was replaced by Fran Tarkenton. In his first NFL game Tarkenton wasted no time. He completed a swing pass to Mel Triplett on his first pass and connected on his next three passes. Two minutes into the second quarter, Tarkenton hit Bob Schnelker for a 14-yard touchdown to put Minnesota up by ten points. Chicago closed the gap to 10-6 by the half. In the third quarter linebacker Rip Hawkins, the Vikings' number-two pick in the college draft out of North Carolina, smashed into Willie Galimore, who fumbled. The Vikings recovered, and two plays later Tarkenton lofted a 29-yard pass to Jerry Reichow, whom the Vikings had acquired from the Washington Redskins just a few days before the season opened. Another rookie who had a good game was Tommy Mason, the team's top pick in the collegiate draft. He was from Tulane University in New Orleans, and since Hawkins was from North Carolina and Tarkenton, the Vikings' third draft choice, was from Georgia, the trio of top picks was known as the Three Rebels. Tarkenton was the star of that game. Throughout the game he changed the play with audibles at the line of scrimmage to keep the Bear defense off balance. He completed 17 of 23 passes for 250 yards, and he passed for four touchdowns and ran for another, giving the Vikings a decisive 37-13 victory.

Those early years of the Vikings were a lot of fun. My color analyst for the games on CBS was Clayton Tonnemaker, a local legend. He had played at Edison High School in Minneapolis and then was one of the leaders of the University of Minnesota Gopher football squad in 1949, the last great team under coach Bernie Bierman. Tonnemaker later played for the Green Bay Packers.

Norm Van Brocklin, the Dutchman, as he was called, could be very charming one minute and then explode the next. Sometimes he seemed to think the reporters would never understand what he was trying to say, but he and the other coaches were very helpful to me. Van Brocklin did an outstanding job of organizing a team's offense, but Fran Tarkenton's scrambling tactics drove him batty. During his years as a player, Van Brocklin had been a classic drop-back quarterback, whereas Tarkenton in those early years was known as the Scrambler. The Vikings offensive line wasn't very good when the team was new, and Tarkenton wouldn't have been able to count on much pass protection had he been a straight drop-back passer. Later in his career, when he had better lines in front of him, Tarkenton became a more conventional quarterback. Van Brocklin thought Tarkenton's scrambling caused the pass patterns to break down like the Keystone Kops running all over the field. On the other hand, the fans loved the scrambling. Fran Tarkenton quickly became one of the most exciting quarterbacks in the league.

Even with the big win over the Bears in their first game,

the Vikings won just five games their first two seasons. They let some leads slip away. In their third game of the 1961 season, the Vikings took a 33-31 lead at Baltimore on Mike Mercer's fourth field goal of the game with just 30 seconds left to play. But after the kickoff, the Colts' Johnny Unitas fired a long pass to Lenny Moore, who grabbed it and stepped out of bounds at the Minnesota 44 with just one second left on the clock. Then Steve Myhra came out to try a 52-yard field goal (the goal posts then were on the goal line and not at the back of the end zone like they are now). Myhra's kick cleared the crossbar as time expired and the Colts pulled it out, 34-33, a heartbreaking loss for the Vikings.

In 1962 the Steelers pulled out a win on a late field goal by Lou Michaels, a left-footed kicker, who also played defensive end. In addition to three field goals and four points-after, he even had a safety. Back then the kickers weren't the specialists they are today. It wasn't unusual for a team's kicker to hold down another position on the team. This was the only time I was ever at Forbes Field, which is better remembered as the home of the Pittsburgh Pirates. It was one of the classic baseball stadiums. Set up for football that day, the place seemed pretty empty with an attendance of only 14,600, the smallest crowd ever to watch the Vikings in a regular-season game, home or away.

The week after the loss to the Steelers came another heartbreaker in a game against the Chicago Bears at Wrigley Field, another classic baseball stadium that was used for football for many years. In the first half the Vikings were trailing by four and backed up to their own 11-yard line, when Tarkenton lofted a long pass down the right sideline to Charley Ferguson. He outwrestled Bennie McRae for the catch, broke a tackle, and then outraced Richie Petitbon down the right sideline for an 89-yard touchdown, still the longest pass from scrimmage in Viking history. This play helped Minnesota cling to a 30-28 lead late in the game, and when the Vikings intercepted a Billy Wade pass with 30 seconds left, all they had to do was run out the clock. Instead, they fumbled, and the Bears recovered. A few seconds later, as the clock was winding down, Roger Leclerc kicked a game-winning field goal for the Bears.

The Vikings and Packers have always had a great rivalry. Because the Green Bay Packers were from a neighboring state, a lot of Wisconsin fans were in the stands whenever they played at Met Stadium. Minnesota fans were very familiar with the Packers, because the Packers had been like the home team to most people in Minnesota before the advent of the Vikings. Of course, in the early years the Viking-Packer games were a mismatch, since the Packers were in some of their greatest years under coach Vince Lombardi. In their first four games the closest the Vikings came to the Packers was an 18-point loss in 1961.

In their fifth game, at Minnesota in October 1963, Bart Starr had three touchdown passes, and the Packers led, 27-7, in the third quarter. But the Vikings defense came through with some big plays, and Fran Tarkenton started picking apart the Green Bay secondary. Herb Adderley, the Packers' great cornerback, was having a rough day. He let Paul Flatley get by him for a 29-yard touchdown pass in the third quarter. Then, late in the game with the Packers up by only 30-27, Adderley missed a tackle at midfield, allowing Flatley to run all the way to the Packer ten-yard line.

The Minnesota fans were really excited now. The Vikings advanced to the three and brought the field goal team in on fourth down, right at the two-minute warning. The Vikings were on the verge of beating the world-champion Packers. All Fred Cox had to do was kick a ten-yard field goal. Tarkenton would be the holder for Cox. Just before the ball was snapped, Herb Adderley shifted sides in the Green Bay backfield, flooding the right side for the Packers. There was no one to block him, and he got a great jump when the ball was snapped. Cox got off the kick, but Adderley dived in front of it, blocking it cleanly with his face mask. The ball caromed in front of the Packers' Hank Gremminger, who scooped it up and rumbled 80 yards in the other direction for a touchdown. Instead of winning, 31-30, the Vikings lost, 37-28.

The first time the Packers and Vikings met in the 1964 season, at Lambeau Field in Green Bay, they had another great game. Each team scored a pair of touchdowns in the second quarter. Thanks to Rip Hawkins, who blocked one of Paul Hornung's extra-point attempts, the Vikings had a one-point lead. The lead seesawed back and forth in the second half. Green Bay had a 23-21 lead as the Vikings took possession of the ball on their own 20 with less than two minutes to play.

The Vikings quickly advanced to near midfield but then stalled. On fourth down they were at their 36-yard line with 22 yards needed for a first down. The Packers would be playing to protect against a long pass, but behind the line of scrimmage Tarkenton danced and eluded the Packers until his receivers could break away from their defenders. Tarkenton spotted Tom Hall downfield and heaved a pass in his direction. Meanwhile, another Vikings end, Gordie Smith, was racing toward the ball, not realizing the pass was not meant for him. Hall was wide open and it looked like Smith might end up breaking up the play. Instead, Smith grabbed the pass while moving full tilt at around the Packer 35 and chugged all the way down to the 21-yard line. Minnesota ran one more play to position the ball in the center of the field and sent in Fred Cox with 18 seconds left. This time nobody got through to block the ball, and Cox kicked the winning field goal. The Vikings finally had a victory over the mighty Packers.

My final season covering the Vikings, in 1964, included the most bizarre play I've ever seen. At Kezar Stadium against the 49ers, the Vikings opened up a 27-17 lead when rookie Carl Eller recovered a fumble and ran 45 yards with it for a touchdown. On San Francisco's next possession George Mira completed a pass to Bill Kilmer. Three Vikings converged on Kilmer and the ball squirted loose, right in front of defensive end Jim Marshall. Marshall scooped up the ball at the San Francisco 34-yard line and took off— toward the wrong end zone. At first he seemed to be taking a few steps in that direction to get clear of traffic. Ed Sharockman, the nearest Viking to Marshall, turned to start blocking in the other direction. But Marshall never turned around.

I was shouting into the mike, "He's running the wrong way! He's running the wrong way!" The Viking bench was across the field from my broadcast booth, and I could see them frantically waving and shouting, but Marshall couldn't hear them over the roar of the crowd. Behind him ran 49er guard Bruce Bosely, ready to block anyone—friend or foe—who attempted to stop Marshall on his way to the wrong end zone. After Marshall crossed the goal line and flung the ball away (completely out of bounds so it ended up as a safety), Bosely patted him on the shoulder pads. When he figured out what happened, Marshall bent over and buried his head in his hands.

Marshall had rushed the passer all the way back to the goal line and then turned in the other direction as Mira scrambled back toward the line of scrimmage. After the pass was completed to Billy Kilmer, Marshall hustled upfield to help with the tackle. By the time the ball came loose, he wasn't sure which way he was going anymore. In the 1929

Rose Bowl, Roy Riegels of California ran the wrong way, a play that resulted in his team losing to Georgia Tech. I'm surprised it doesn't happen more often.

Jim was really disconsolate after the game. The other Vikings kidded him but also reminded him that, despite the wrong-way run, he had played a great game. After all, it was Marshall's hard hit on Mira that had forced the fumble that Eller ran back for a touchdown. H. P. Skoglund, one of the Vikings' owners, came into the locker room and told Jim that he had done the same thing in a college game for St. Olaf. Skoglund's teammates tackled him after he had run 40 yards. That story seemed to cheer Marshall up.

On the team bus taking us to the airport after the game, Marshall sat next to me. I still wasn't sure how he was feeling, so I didn't say a word. After a while Jim asked me, "Do you think people will ever forget this?"

"I don't know, Jim," I said. "A lot of people will forget it, and some will remember. But don't forget, they'll also remember your great plays, including some in the game today. It's just one of those things. It's happened before. Just be glad that you had a great game today—and that the Vikings won."

In the following weeks Marshall received a lot of fan mail and letters of support. One of them was from Roy Riegels, the University of California player who had done the same thing more than 30 years before.

The Vikings made progress in 1964. One of their great new stars was defensive end Carl Eller from the University of Minnesota. Eller wanted to play with the Vikings, so he threatened that if any NFL team other than the Vikings drafted him, he might play in the American Football League instead. Eventually the two rival leagues merged, but in the early years of the AFL, when the two leagues held separate collegiate drafts, the players had more options. In 1963, in fact, the Vikings had lost in their bid for University of Minnesota defensive star Bobby Bell, who signed with the AFL Kansas City Chiefs. And Fran Tarkenton had been drafted by the AFL Boston Patriots, who offered him more money, but Fran preferred the Vikings and the NFL.

The Vikings themselves almost entered the American Football League. Minneapolis had been granted a franchise for the AFL's first season of 1960, but Minnesota was awarded a National Football League franchise to start in 1961, and the AFL team granted to the Twin Cities was instead given to Oakland, creating the Raiders. Max Winter told me once that when he was raising the money for a professional football franchise for Minnesota, he found it very difficult to find half a dozen people willing to invest $50,000 each. Max said he couldn't believe how difficult it was getting investors to put up the money. Of course, in those days, there probably weren't too many people like Max, who could actually foresee how these football franchises would increase in value over the years.

The Vikings had their first winning season in 1964, with a record of 8-5-1. After they beat the Bears, 41-14, in the final game of the regular season, they had a chance to be in a post-season game—the Playoff Bowl, which matched up the second-place finishers in each division. If the Packers lost to the Rams in their final game, the Packers would finish in third place at 8-6. In the Packers-Rams game, which was still in progress when the Vikings finished their game at Chicago, the Rams led by 14 points in the fourth quarter, but the Packers scored two touchdowns to tie the game and finish the season at 8-5-1, the same record as the Vikings. Because they had scored more points in their two games with the Vikings that year, the Packers went to the Playoff Bowl. Van Brocklin was miffed by this tie-breaking system, but I don't know how else they could have made the decision, other than flipping a coin.

In the spring of 1965, while I was down in Florida with the Twins, one of Bill MacPhail's assistants at CBS informed me that I would no longer be announcing the Vikings' games. The Ford Motor Company, one of the Vikings' primary sponsors, had pressured CBS to give the job to an announcer named Jim Morse, who had an in with somebody at Ford. Just like that, I was out. Jim Morse announced the Vikings' games for one year and was replaced. Meanwhile, Chet Simmons, the sports director at NBC, offered me a chance to announce the AFL games. It didn't take me long to accept. My color analyst was Andy Robustelli, who had just retired the year before after a great career with the Los Angeles Rams and New York Giants. He was eventually elected to the Pro Football Hall of Fame. With NBC I wasn't assigned to any particular team, so I saw a greater variety of games. The AFL in those early years was fun to follow, in their old, often rather small stadiums.

With football announcing I had to miss the Sunday baseball games during the last half of September, so I felt torn on September 26, 1965, when I had to go to Oakland to broadcast the Raiders' game against the Houston Oilers. It was quite a game. Tom Flores threw three touchdown passes for Oakland, including one to win the game in the final minute after the Raiders recovered an Oiler fumble on the Houston 17-yard line. But my mind was elsewhere because that day the Minnesota Twins clinched the American League pennant in Washington, D. C. This was one time I would have rather been back with the baseball team.

Calvin Griffith, the Twins' owner, also wished I had been there. For years, he had contended with the fact that two of his announcers (Ray Scott being the other) were also committed to professional football on Sundays and one or both

I started announcing games for the Springfield Cubs in 1950.

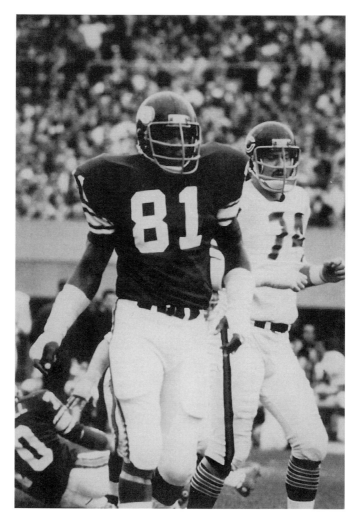

Carl Eller went from the Minnesota Gophers to the Minnesota Vikings. *Minnesota Vikings.*

Rip Hawkins was one of the Three Rebels, along with Tarkenton and Tommy Mason. *Minnesota Vikings.*

Jim Marshall was a great defensive end, although he may be
remembered best for a memorable wrong-way run. *Minnesota Vikings.*

could be missing from the Twins' broadcast. Finally, Calvin went to bat on my behalf and helped me get a better contract with the sponsors, so I could quit the football games and concentrate on baseball. As a result, I announced AFL games for only one year.

I did get permission to do a few college games and did the University of Minnesota Gophers in 1968 and 1969. The Gophers opened their 1968 season at home against the University of Southern California and their great halfback, O. J. Simpson. The Gophers gave USC a real battle, but Simpson rushed for well over 200 yards and four touchdowns, and USC won, 29-20.

The only football I've done since then was for Ohio State, flying on Saturdays to wherever the Buckeyes were playing. The Buckeye coach was Woody Hayes, who always roamed the sidelines in shirtsleeves no matter what the weather. He was also known for his terrible temper. In the game against Michigan in 1971 he blasted the officials several times and even tore up the first-down markers. At that time Ohio State was the top team in the Big Ten. Their final game of the season, always with Michigan, often determined the Big Ten representative in the Rose Bowl.

At the Michigan game at Ohio Stadium in 1972 Michigan came into the game with a 7-0 Big Ten record, while Ohio State was 6-1. Michigan needed to win or tie this game to win the conference title and go to the Rose Bowl in Pasadena, California. If the Buckeyes won, they'd finish in a tie for the Big Ten championship, and most of us figured that Ohio State would then get the Rose Bowl berth for having won this game against Michigan. During the week before the game the Michigan coach, Bo Schembechler, said he would play for a tie if appropriate, since a tie was their ticket to Pasadena.

But during the game he disdained a couple of chances for

a field goal, and Ohio State made several brilliant goal-line stands, denying Michigan a touchdown. Near the end of the first half the Buckeyes stopped Michigan on four successive downs from the one-yard line. In the third quarter a 30-yard touchdown run by Archie Griffin, then a freshman, put Ohio State up by 14-3. Michigan came back with a touchdown and a two-point conversion. They were now only a field goal away from tying. In the fourth quarter they drove down to the one-yard line again. Ohio State held on third down, and again the Wolverines tried again for a touchdown on fourth down. Quarterback Dennis Franklin kept the ball and tried to sneak in, but he was stacked up short of the goal line.

Ohio State won, 14-11, tying Michigan for the Big Ten title, and the next morning the conference athletic directors awarded the Rose Bowl berth to the Buckeyes. In the next two years Michigan and Ohio State again tied for the Big Ten championship, and both times Ohio State received the votes to go to the Rose Bowl.

Another great thing about announcing for the Buckeyes during that time was being able to watch the development of Archie Griffin. Griffin won the Heisman Trophy as a junior in 1974. Then he won it again in 1975, becoming the only player to get the award twice.

Calling the action for Ohio State during the 1970s turned out to be the end of me for football announcing. But it was quite a way to go out.

Part Two

Time with the Twins

This was a familiar sight in the 1960s: Harmon Killebrew
sending one out. *WCCO Radio.*

Catching a Star

When, near the end of the 1961 baseball season, it was becoming evident I wouldn't be back with the Baltimore Orioles for the next season, Bob Wolff, one of the announcers for the Twins, accepted a position with Madison Square Garden in New York, creating an opening in their broadcast booth. I was already slated to be the announcer for CBS Television on all the Viking games in 1961, so it made sense that Art Lund of Campbell-Mithun Advertising, the agency used by the Hamm Brewing Company, would offer me the job announcing for the Twins, once I'd been approved by Hamm's Beer and Calvin Griffith, the owner of the Twins. When I started with the Twins, my paychecks came from Campbell-Mithun, the advertising agency for Hamm's Beer. In 1970 in Minnesota the stations gained more control over the broadcasts, and at that time I became employed by WCCO Radio, and henceforth I did only radio broadcasts, except for some television announcing in 1970. During the time the sponsors were paying my salary, though, the same broadcast crew was on both radio and television. All the games were carried on radio, and at that time the Twins televised 50 games, mostly road games, on WTCN-TV, Channel 11.

My original partners with the Twins were Ray Scott and Halsey Hall. Ray already had a national reputation for announcing the Green Bay Packers on CBS Television, but he had never done any regular baseball announcing before coming to the Twins. Halsey was well known in Minnesota for covering local sports both as a newspaper writer and a broadcaster. Halsey, with his wealth of stories and memories, was the color analyst, while Ray and I shared the play-by-play announcing.

When a game was on both television and radio, Ray or I would do the television announcing while the other would do the radio, and Halsey would move back and forth between us. After four and a half innings Ray and I would trade places. When Ray announced on television for the first half and I then took over from him, I could unwittingly say what he had already said. This problem could have been eliminated if we each announced the entire game on radio or television, alternating media from game to game. When the games were on radio only, Ray and I would again switch halfway through. Sometimes when Ray was on the air, I stepped out of the radio booth, especially the cramped Comiskey Park booth, and watched the game from somewhere else in the press box, but usually we stayed in the booth so one could hear what the other was saying and not repeat the same things when he came back on the air.

Marty O'Neill, an announcer long associated with St. Paul, worked with us on weekends in the early years. Marty was a real legend in the Twin Cities. He had done the play-by-play for St. Paul Saints baseball and hockey for years and had hosted a popular Sunday morning sports show on television. By the time I got to know him, Marty had gotten started in announcing professional wrestling. In fact, when he died in 1983, most people remembered him as a wrestling announcer. In a way, that's too bad because he had done so much more. In his younger years, he was an outstanding athlete at St. Paul Central (and became a charter member of the school's Athletic Hall of Fame in 1995). He played a number of sports but baseball was his best. After high school, he played some amateur ball and was a member of a team that won the world amateur baseball championship in 1939. When he got into radio, he was widely regarded as one of the most knowledgeable baseball announcers around. I really found that to be the case during the chances I had to work with him. He sure knew baseball. Marty was a very pleasant guy, and I thought a lot of him. He and a few others organized a bowling league that I was in. Marty was sort of the unofficial commissioner of that league, which still exists. Kent Hrbek and a few of the other Twins have bowled in that league.

At first I had been a little apprehensive about moving to Minnesota, because I'd done most of my work in the East, and you never know how you're going to be received when you move to another area. But the people in Minnesota proved to be quite tolerant. They gave you a chance to prove yourself before they criticized you much. Kathy and I went to Minnesota in February 1962 and bought a small house in the country-club area of the suburb of Edina. Not far away was a house we'd drive by regularly, and I often thought, "There's a house I'd really like to have." After a year and a half, Tom Thompson, a real estate man we knew, called to tell us about another house for sale in Edina. The house he took us to was the house I liked so much. We bought it and have lived there since 1964.

In 1962, my first season with them, after a record of 70-90 the year before, the Twins were in close contention with the New York Yankees and finished the year in second place, only five games out of first, with a record of 91-71. It was only the second winning season for the franchise since the end of World War II. The Twins drew 1.4 million fans that season. Every other car on the road had a "Win Twins!" bumper sticker. Just about anywhere you went in the Twin

Cities during the season, people were talking about the Twins.

Sam Mele, the manager in 1962, had a standard lineup and batting order. It was unusual then and completely different from current practice. For example, in 1994 the most that Twins' manager Tom Kelly used any one batting order was seven times. Mele's regular batting order made it easy for me to fill out my scorebook before each game:

Lenny Green, cf
Vic Power, 1b
Rich Rollins, 3b
Harmon Killebrew, lf
Bob Allison, rf
Earl Battey, c
Bernie Allen, 2b
Zoilo Versalles, ss

From game to game little changed except the pitcher, who hit in the ninth spot.

Lenny Green, whom I'd known in Baltimore, was speedy, well suited to play center field and be the lead-off batter.

Vic Power had come to the Twins, along with left-handed pitcher Dick Stigman, in a trade with the Indians just before the season opened. Vic was a very slick fielder. He could play any position in the infield, although first base was his usual position. He'd always catch pop-ups one-handed, which drove Little League coaches crazy. They'd tell the kids to catch always with two hands, but the kids imitated Vic.

Rich Rollins and Bernie Allen, newcomers that year— Allen officially a rookie and Rollins a virtual rookie—did great. Rollins had a .298 batting average with 96 runs batted in, more than Roger Maris that year.

Earl Battey was one of the best catchers in the American

League throughout much of the 1960s, and he was a fine hitter too. He won the American League Gold Glove Award for catchers for the third straight year in 1962. He was extremely good at picking runners off base, especially runners on third.

Zoilo Versalles led American League shortstops in double plays in 1962. He also hit 17 home runs, a good total for a shortstop. Zoilo eventually moved from the eighth spot in the batting order to the lead-off position.

The biggest stars in those early years were Harmon Killebrew and Bob Allison. In a game against the Indians in July 1962 Allison and Killebrew each hit a grand slam—in the same inning. Allison was the American League Rookie of the Year in 1959 when he hit 30 home runs for the Washington Senators and had many great seasons after the Senators became the Twins. In 1961 and 1962 he topped 100 RBIs. He was a great right fielder with a strong and deadly accurate right arm. Whenever Allison had the ball, runners were wary about taking an extra base or tagging up and advancing after a fly. A former fullback at Kansas University, Bob could crash into catchers blocking the plate the way he used to crash into linebackers. Once he collided with Chicago catcher Duane Josephson so hard that Josephson's glove flew off and sailed two rows into the stands. His teammates used to call him Mr. America, but to me he was Mr. Indestructible. So it was a shock when, in the late 1980s, he developed ataxia, a disease that attacks the muscles. Bob died just before the opening of the 1995 baseball season. I'll always remember how good he looked in his blue pinstriped uniform with the big number 4 on his back.

Harmon Killebrew was the best the Twins have ever had. He hit 46 home runs in 1961 and 48 in 1962, the third time he topped 40 home runs, and he would top 40 five more times. In 1962 he hit 11 home runs in his last 12 games, and besides leading the league with 48 home runs, he also led with 126 RBIs. In fact, when the season ended, Harmon led the majors, not just the American League, in home runs. In the National League, Willie Mays had 47 home runs. But Mays' team, the San Francisco Giants, had finished in a first-place tie with the Los Angeles Dodgers and then had a three-game playoff. Those three games were counted as part of the regular season, so when Mays hit two home runs in those games, he passed Harmon as the major-league leader. I always thought it was a little unfair for Killebrew to be denied that way, but he later led the major leagues a couple of times. In 1962 Killebrew also set a major-league record (which has since then been broken many times) by striking out 142 times. Killebrew refined his batting eye in the following years and became an even more dangerous hitter— as if a guy who hits 48 home runs isn't already dangerous enough.

Although the Twins were best known for their hitting in 1962, they did have some good pitchers. Lefty Jim Kaat won 18 games, and two other southpaws, Jack Kralick and Dick Stigman, each won 12 and had winning records. The only right-hander in the rotation was the outstanding Camilo Pascual. Pascual had one of the best curveballs anybody had ever seen, and when Bert Blyleven came up with the Twins in 1970 with his great curve, everyone compared it to Pascual's. Pascual won 20 games in 1962 and led the league with 206 strikeouts, despite an inflamed tendon in his arm that at one point limited him to just two starts over a one-month span. Camilo got his 20th win in the Twins' final game of the year. He went the distance on a three-hitter, struck out seven, and hurled his fifth shutout of the season as the Twins beat Baltimore, 1-0. Killebrew drove in the only run of the game in the first inning. It was a good way for the

Twins to cap a great season for them and for me to finish out my first season with the team.

While 1962 was a great year all around, the highlight of the season came on Sunday, August 26. The Twins were completing a three-game series against the Kansas City Athletics, and Jack Kralick was on the mound, facing Bill Fischer of the A's. Kralick had been pitching well for the Twins in the month before. He had won his last three decisions to up his season record to 9-8. In his last outing he had a no-hitter going against the Senators for 5 1/3 innings. Not an overpowering hurler, Jack pitched with finesse.

In this game Kralick relied mainly on his fastball and slider. The first two batters of the game for Kansas City, Bobby Del Greco and Ed Charles, hit the ball hard. Del Greco had led off the previous day's game with a home run, and for a moment his long drive to left-center looked like another homer, but the wind held it in the park, and it was caught. Ed Charles then hit a long shot to right, but the wind again held it up, and Allison made the catch. After that, the Athletics didn't come close to getting a man on base until the fourth inning, when Charles came up again and hit another long one to right. Allison made a spectacular leaping backhanded catch at the fence in front of the bullpen in right-center field. Kralick kept mowing them down and had retired all the batters he had faced through seven innings. But Bill Fischer of the A's was nearly as tough, and the game was scoreless until in the last of the seventh when the Twins pushed a run across and took a 1-0 lead. In the eighth inning Kralick retired Norm Siebern, Gino Cimoli, and Manny Jimenez. No-hitters are not common, but Kralick was on the verge of something extremely rare: a perfect game in which no batter reaches first base safely by any means—hit, walk, error, or anything else.

Wayne Causey led off the ninth for Kansas City and hit a

ball down the left-field line that finally sliced foul. Causey then grounded out to Bernie Allen, and Kralick was just two outs away. Catcher Bill Bryan was the next scheduled batter but he was called back, and out of the dugout came a player with the name Turk on his back. Most of the A's had their last names on their uniforms, but team owner Charlie Finley occasionally used the player's nickname. Turk was George Alusik, a right-handed batter, definitely a threat to break up a no-hitter. Kralick worked carefully, starting with a ball and then a strike. The next two pitches were out of the strike zone. Alusik then fouled off a pitch. The stadium was pretty quiet as Jack came in with the 3-2 pitch. It was high and outside. Alusik had walked to become the Athletics' first base runner of the game.

The perfect game had been broken up, but Kralick still had a shot at a no-hitter. Billy Consolo, a former Twin, pinch hit for Fischer and popped out to Vic Power in foul territory. Bobby Del Greco, the leadoff batter, then lifted another high pop in foul territory on the first-base side. Once again Power drifted over and, one-handed as usual, made the catch. Kralick had his no-hitter and there was pandemonium on the field. The Twins, in their second season in Minnesota, had produced a no-hitter. It would be more than 30 years before another nine-inning no-hitter would be pitched in Minnesota.

Probably the most notable Twins player in 1963 was right-handed relief pitcher Bill Dailey, whom the Twins purchased from the Cleveland Indians the day before the season opened. Dailey had had a brief and rather undistinguished career in the majors. The Twins used him out of the bullpen, and there was nothing spectacular about his performance during the first few weeks of the season. But then Mele began using him to protect leads late in the game, and Dailey proved to be very effective. Today's "closer" might pitch just the final inning of a game, but in the 1960s the late-inning relievers were more like firemen. They'd often be brought into the middle of a jam to try to work their way out of an inning without allowing any of the baserunners to score. They often came in during the sixth or seventh inning and then went the rest of the way. Dailey proved to be outstanding in this role in 1963. Although saves weren't an official statistic then, Dailey did protect leads in 21 of the games he finished, in addition to winning six of nine decisions with an ERA of 1.99.

The fans loved Dailey, and whenever he was brought in, Willie Peterson, the Met Stadium organist, would play, "Won't You Come Home, Bill Bailey?" Of course, in this case, it was "Won't You Come Home, Bill Dailey?" Dailey received the Joseph W. Haynes Award as the Twins' Pitcher of the Year, even though Camilo Pascual had come through with another 20-win season. Dailey had arm problems in 1964 and wasn't effective. He pitched in only 14 games, and that was the end of his career in the majors.

Another reliever for the Twins in 1963 was Ray "Old Blue" Moore. He had been a good starting pitcher with the St. Paul Saints in the early 1950s. I also knew him when he pitched for Baltimore for a few years. His nickname came from his hunting dog called Old Blue. After the baseball season he and Old Blue spent the winter coon hunting. One of the other Oriole pitchers, Connie Johnson, had a hunting dog named Sport, and they were always arguing who had the better dog.

"Does your dog ever call you when you're on the road?" Connie asked. "Mine does."

"No," Ray replied, "but can yours swim on his back? Old Blue can do the backstroke."

Ray had more stories about that dog of his. He said once Old Blue had thought they were going hunting, but when

Ray picked up his fishing rod instead, Old Blue started digging for worms. Moore was used almost exclusively in relief by the Twins his three years in Minnesota and was pretty good for the first two. In 1963, however, it was clear he was near the end. That same year, the Twins acquired another veteran, Wally Post, a great power hitter for many seasons with the Cincinnati Reds. Wally usually got along with Ray but didn't like the pipe that Ray was always smoking, even on the team bus. Whenever Wally asked him not to smoke on the bus, Ray told him to sit somewhere else. One day Wally grabbed the pipe right out of Moore's mouth and threw it out the bus window. Ray didn't say a word, but a little later he took out a penknife and sliced off part of Wally's pants.

Nobody heard much from Moore after he left baseball at the end of the 1963 season. When I asked his brother, called Jughead, whatever happened to Ray, Jughead said, "He's doing what he's always done. He's going coon hunting." Ray died in March 1995, but I didn't learn of his death until six weeks later.

Another reclusive player, Jimmie Hall, was in his first season in 1963. Jimmie had such broad shoulders that everyone called him Wedge. He came from North Carolina, and, last I heard, that's where he is now, but nobody's seen him since he retired. Once when I said to him at the end of the season, "Jim, I'll be seeing you around," he replied, "No, you won't be seeing me anymore." Jimmie played center field and quickly took the job away from Lenny Green. A left-handed batter, Hall hit 33 home runs, breaking Ted Williams' record for most home runs by a first-year player in the American League.

In 1963, along with Hall's 33 home runs, Bob Allison had 35, and Earl Battey hit 26, his career high. Killebrew, of course, finished ahead of everyone with 45 home runs, even

78

though he missed much of the first six weeks of the year after wrenching his knee in spring training. That year the Twins hit 225 homers, the second-highest total ever hit by any team in the majors.

There was an innovation at the Met in 1963: the Twins were the first team to measure the distances of home runs. Len Meffert, the educational director at the state prison at Stillwater, measured the fence lines and angles at Metropolitan Stadium and correlated them to determine the distance from home plate to any point beyond the outfield fences. Tom Mee, the Twins' public-relations director, handled the system during games, quickly announcing the distance of every home run. Nowadays at the Metrodome the Twins also take into account the trajectory of the drive in order to estimate how far it would have traveled unimpeded. At the Met a homer announced as 400 feet actually landed at a spot 400 feet away, whereas at the Metrodome a 400-foot measurement means that the ball would have landed at 400 feet if it hadn't hit the seats or whatever else.

The Twins won 91 games in 1963 and finished in third place. They led the American League with attendance of 1,406,652. The Twins had a powerful club during these early years in Minnesota, and they often broke out in a barrage of home runs. In one game of a doubleheader in Washington during the 1963 season they tied a major-league record by hitting eight home runs in one game. And they hit four home runs in the other game of that doubleheader. Three years later they hit five homers in one inning at Met Stadium in a game against the Kansas City Athletics.

The biggest burst I recall was in Kansas City on a Saturday night in May 1964. The Twins and A's were tied in the tenth inning when Tony Oliva homered off Dan Pfister to break the tie. Bob Allison then followed with a homer, and Jimmie Hall made it three in a row. The A's brought in Vern

Handrahan to pitch. Killebrew, who had homered earlier in the game, then homered to left for the Twins' fourth home run in a row, tying the major-league record.

Meanwhile, in another booth in the press box a strange drama was unfolding. Charlie Finley, the A's owner, in Louisville for the Kentucky Derby, had phoned Jim Schaaf, the A's public-relations director, to find out how the game was coming. Finley called just as Oliva was stepping into the batter's box in the tenth.

Schaaf reported Oliva's home run as it happened. Finley's mood worsened as Hall's home run was described. When Schaaf then told him Allison had hit one out, Finley started to doubt him. "You better not be kidding me," he threatened Schaaf.

Schaaf assured his boss he was telling the truth as the A's changed pitchers. But Killebrew's home run was too much for Finley to believe. In fact, he was so convinced that Schaaf was pulling his leg that he fired him over the phone. Of course, when he checked the sports section the next morning, he had no choice to call back and rehire him.

This year, 1964, was the first full season for Tony Oliva. He had been in the Twins organization since 1961 and had made his major-league debut in September 1962 by getting two hits, a single and a double, off a couple of pretty good pitchers for Cleveland: Dick Donovan, who won 20 games that year, and Sam McDowell, a rookie who went on to some great seasons with the Indians. Tony played only nine games with the Twins in 1962 and seven the next year, and even though he had hit well in the minors, the Twins didn't seem to think he would make the grade at the major-league level. They were thinking about releasing him, but Phil Howser, the Twins' farm director, decided to hang onto him. Then in 1964, his rookie season, Oliva led the American

League in hits, runs scored, and batting average. He won the batting crown his first two years in the league and once again later in his career. Allison was moved to first base in 1964 to make room for Oliva in right field. In his early years Tony had some problems in the outfield, especially with judging the distance of fly balls, but he kept improving. He had such a strong arm that eventually he was regarded as one of the best outfielders in the game. He played 15 seasons with Minnesota and was one of the best Twins ever, along with Killebrew, Carew, Hrbek, and Puckett.

The Twins had another powerful club in 1964. They led the league in runs scored for the second straight year, and with 221 home runs they nearly duplicated their total from the year before. Don Mincher, a reserve first baseman, hit 23 homers despite his limited playing time. The others with 20 or more home runs were Bob Allison, Zoilo Versalles, Tony Oliva, Jimmie Hall, and Harmon Killebrew, who led the American League with 49. In 1964 the Twins scored nearly 60 runs more than their opponents, but they finished the season four games under .500 in a tie for sixth place.

The Twins' relief pitching had fallen apart in the first half of the season and their defense in the second half. Bill Dailey hurt his arm in spring training and couldn't repeat his 1963 magic. The acquisition of veteran pitchers Al Worthington and Johnny Klippstein bolstered the bullpen, but the Twins led the American League in complete games, an indication of how little they could rely on their relief pitching. Their top starter was Jim Kaat, who won 17 games. Camilo Pascual won 15, and Jim "Mudcat" Grant was 11-9 with an ERA of 2.82, after coming to the Twins in a midseason deal with Cleveland. Mudcat was one of those pitchers the Twins always had trouble beating. That might have been one of the reasons they made the trade, so they wouldn't have to face him anymore. Whatever the reason, it turned out to be a good move for Minnesota.

The Twins' most outstanding pitching performance in 1964 was in June in the first game of a doubleheader at the Met against Chicago. Left-hander Gerry Arrigo set down the White Sox without a hit through the first eight innings. The only runners he allowed were on a walk and a couple of hit batsmen. Arrigo had grown up in Chicago, not far from Comiskey Park, and had been originally signed by the White Sox. The first batter to face him in the ninth was Mike Hershberger, a former teammate in winter ball. Jerry had been getting Hershberger out on sliders, but he came in with a fastball on the second pitch. Hershberger lined it over the head of the second baseman Jerry Kindall and into right center for a base hit. Arrigo still finished the game with a one-hit shutout.

Gerry was a nice young man but a little offbeat. During the 1964 season we were in Cleveland when President Lyndon Johnson was visiting the city, and Arrigo went shopping for a gift for his child back home. He bought a push toy with a long handle. When he came out of the store with it in a big long box, he saw the president's motorcade and worked his way through the crowd to the curb for a close look. Sure enough, he was apprehended by the Secret Service, who thought he might have a weapon in that box of his.

I guess that could have happened to anyone, but somehow Arrigo seemed to gravitate toward that kind of a jam. Arno Goethel, a St. Paul newspaper reporter, said he once asked Arrigo why left-handers were eccentric.

"That's a lot of baloney," Gerry replied. "Left-handers aren't any different from anybody else."

At the end of the interview Arrigo got up to leave, turned around, and walked into a closet.

So 1964 was an exciting year, though a bit of a downer for the Twins. But the enthusiasm was still there, and people in the Upper Midwest loved the Twins no matter how they did. It made you wonder how crazy the fans would get if the Twins could break through and do something really great.

My original partners on Twins broadcasts were Halsey Hall and
Ray Scott. What a pair. *WCCO Radio*.

When the World
Came to Minnesota

At the beginning of the 1965 season there was optimism in Minnesota, and the Twins were about to lead the league in attendance, with more than 1.4 million fans. But the Yankees were still there. They had won the American League pennant for the last five years, in 14 of the last 16 years. From 1921 through 1964 the Yankees had won 29 pennants and 20 World Series. During this period they had never gone more than three years without winning the pennant. But the greatest dynasty in the history of sports was about to end. In 1965 the Yankees dropped to sixth place, finishing eight games below .500. Some of their great players were declining. Mickey Mantle, who had hit .303 with 35 home runs and 111 RBIs the year before, dropped to 19 homers and only 46 runs batted in, while his batting average nose-dived by nearly 50 points. Roger Maris went from 26 to eight home runs. Joe Pepitone, Bobby Richardson, Tony Kubek, and Elston Howard also dipped in performance. Of that group only Pepitone had any good years left in him. In 1966 the Yankees finished last and didn't win another pennant until 1976. Even though they became a strong team again in the late 1970s and 1980s, they never again achieved their former dominance. In my opinion that was good for baseball.

The Twins were ready for a great year. Their home-run

output dropped to 150 in 1965, a good total but less than the Twins fans had been used to. But the Twins led the American League with 774 runs, almost 100 more than Detroit in second place. With improved fielding in 1965, the Twins finished second in the league in double plays. In 1965 the Twins had a winning record against every team except the Cleveland Indians. They loved to play the Boston Red Sox. In those days, teams played one another 18 times during the season: three different series at home and three on the road. Of their 18 games against the Red Sox, the Twins won 17.

Sam Mele usually went with a set lineup. Battey did most of the catching and was backed up by Jerry Zimmerman. Killebrew had moved in from left field to play first base. Don Mincher filled in at first base during a period when Killebrew was injured and did so well that when Harmon returned, Mincher stayed at first base full-time, and Harmon moved to third in place of Rich Rollins. At first base Mincher had an unorthodox fielding style: he was right-handed, but he kept his left foot on the base when taking throws from the infielders, the opposite of the usual way, but he did a good job there and hit 22 home runs in just 346 at-bats that year. At second base Jerry Kindall, with his fine glove, was the starter most of the year, but Frank Quilici, with the better bat, had the position by the end of the season. At shortstop, of course, Versalles was having an outstanding year. In the outfield, Oliva was in right. Bob Allison was playing his third position in three years: after several years as one of the premier right fielders in the league, known for his strong and accurate arm, Allison was moved to first base in 1964, and then in 1965 he played left field. Sandy Valdespino, who batted left-handed, also played left field on occasion. In center field Jimmie Hall was developing into an outstanding player. Joe Nossek, not a great hitter but a fine outfielder, was often used as a late-inning defensive replacement.

The Twins' pitching improved greatly, thanks mainly to Johnny Sain, who joined the team as its pitching coach that year. The pitchers really loved Sain, who took care of those pitchers like a mother hen. He told them not to talk about any new pitch they were working on: "Don't say anything to the news media about it because, you never know, the word might get around." If a batter had heard about the new pitch, he might be ready for it. Also, Sain didn't believe pitchers needed to do a lot of running between starts, which made him even more popular with the pitchers, who, of course, were never fond of running. Johnny used to say that a person didn't pitch with his legs but with his arm and his head. He said if running were so important, Jesse Owens could have won 30 games. I could never understand that thinking. Strong legs from running ought to help prevent fatigue on the mound, and power pitchers really push off the mound with their legs. I don't think Sain and Sam Mele saw eye to eye about some of Sain's ideas, and Sain was never very close with any manager he worked with throughout his career as a coach.

But Sain's ideas seemed to work with the Twins in 1965. Mudcat Grant had a career year, winning 21 and losing only 7. Jim Kaat was 17-11, and Camilo Pascual, although injured part of the year, was 9-3. Jim Perry was 5-0 in relief appearances and 12-7 overall. The mainstays of the bullpen, Al Worthington and Johnny Klippstein, had a combined record of 19-10 with an earned-run average of well under three runs per game. And that year they also had Dave Boswell, Jim Merritt, Dick Stigman, all of whom could start, and reliever Shorty Pleis.

At spring training in 1965 Sam Mele and Zoilo Versalles got into a bit of a rhubarb, and Sam slapped a $300 fine on

Zoilo for lackadaisical effort. But once the season started Zoilo wasn't lackadaisical. He led the league in doubles with 45, triples with 12, and runs scored with 126. He had a batting average of .273, stole 27 bases, and played in all but two of the Twins games. He did everything that a team could expect of a leadoff hitter. I don't think I ever saw anyone else cover so much ground at shortstop, although he could fumble an easy grounder or hurry a throw needlessly. And sometimes he liked to add a little bit of show to a play. That year Zoilo was voted the American League's Most Valuable Player, the first Twin—and still one of only three—ever to receive the honor. It's sad, but like Allison, Zoilo died at an early age. He was 55 when he died of a heart attack in 1995, only about two months after Bob had passed on.

In the 1965 season a lot of games went down to the wire, and it seemed like the Twins almost always pulled them out, so when the season was over, Ray Scott, Halsey Hall, and I made a highlight album called *Last of the Ninth*. In fact, the season opened at Met Stadium with a win in the last of the twelfth. The Twins were on the verge of defeating the Yankees in the top of the ninth, leading 4-3 with two out and a Yankee runner on second. Joe Pepitone then lifted a pop-up in the infield. Cesar Tovar, making his major-league debut and playing third in place of Rich Rollins, dropped the ball, and Art Lopez, running for Mantle, came around to score and tie the game. But Cesar redeemed himself in the twelfth inning when he lined a two-out single to center to score Bob Allison with the winning run.

Cesar had come to the Twins in an off-season deal that sent Gerry Arrigo to the Cincinnati Reds. At first some Twins fans didn't think much of the deal, but it turned out one of the best trades that the Twins and Calvin Griffith ever made. Tovar became one of the best lead-off hitters around and one of the league's most versatile players—in 1968 he played all nine positions in a single game.

Jim Kaat pitched a fine game in the opener and would have been the winning pitcher if not for Tovar's error. For Kaat just getting to the stadium was a difficult task at the time. He lived in Burnsville, south of the Minnesota River, which had flooded during the huge spring floods that year. The Cedar Avenue Bridge was under water, so Kaat, along with pitcher Dick Stigman and infielders Bill Bethea and Rich Rollins, was shuttled to the Met by helicopter.

A little later in the season, on a weeknight in June, Kaat was involved in an unusual incident in a game with the Cleveland Indians at the Met. He was in a duel with Cleveland's Ralph Terry, who had had some good seasons with the Yankees earlier in the 1960s. The Twins pushed across a run off Terry in the last of the eighth, giving Kaat a 1-0 lead into the ninth. Kaat got one out and was facing slugger Rocky Colavito when the Indians' manager, Birdie Tebbetts, complained to the umpires that Kaat had a hole in the sleeve of his undershirt and, not only that, one of the sleeves was shorter than the other. The umpires ordered Kaat to trim his sleeves to equal lengths, so he went back to the dugout, where trainer George "Doc" Lentz sheared one of his sleeves. Kaat had been pitching great, but he then walked Colavito and gave up a home run to Max Alvis, and the Indians went on to win the game, 2-1.

It was Ralph Terry's 100th career win, but he seemed a little embarrassed to get it this way. Meanwhile, Sam Mele was seething at Tebbetts' tactics. We found out later that the Indians had first spotted the hole in Kaat's shirt in the first inning but had waited until the ninth inning to complain, presumably figuring they might upset Kaat when the game was on the line. Kitty was good-natured about the whole thing. Afterward, one of his Clover Leaf Milk commercials showed Jim saying to one of his kids, "Remember, son, if you're going to be a good pitcher, you have to dress well."

That was a late-inning loss for the Twins, but they had more than their share of late-inning wins. Here are some of them:

In late June the Twins were tied with Detroit in the last of the ninth with two out, the bases loaded, and big Fred Gladding on the mound for the Tigers. Joe Nossek hit a little nubber toward second base. Jerry Lumpe charged in, grabbed the ball, and threw to first, but Nossek beat it out, and the winning run scored.

Later that summer, a game with the Orioles was tied in the last of the eleventh. Tony Oliva was on second, and another runner was on first, with one out. Stu Miller, a deceptive right-hander, got the batter to hit an infield grounder. The Orioles made the force out at second but were too late for a double play at first. As Boog Powell was taking the throw at first, Oliva tore around third and kept going. Powell hesitated just a moment, in disbelief that Tony was trying to score all the way from second, and threw home too late. Oliva slid in with the winning run.

Just a couple days later, in that same series, Baltimore came back in the ninth when Dick Brown hit a three-run homer to tie the game. But in the bottom of the ninth Jimmie Hall homered to the opposite field, and the Twins won, 6-5.

Right after the Baltimore series, the Washington Senators came to the Met and held a 3-2 lead over the Twins in the last of the ninth. Then Jerry Kindall, a good fielder but not a very powerful hitter, picked a good time to hit one of his rare home runs. That tied the game, and soon after Jimmie Hall singled home Versalles to win it. These close games were nerve-racking, and after this one Halsey Hall asked me on the air, "Are you going to make this next trip in a basket or a wheelchair?"

Going into July 1965 five teams were racing neck and neck within a span of only four games: the Twins, White Sox, Indians, Orioles, and Tigers. Then the Twins got hot. They opened the month with nine wins in a row and took over first place for good on July 5. A few days later the Yankees stopped the winning streak.

The next day, the last game before the All-Star break, the Yankees and Twins were tied, 4-4, at the end of the eighth inning. In the top of the ninth the Yankees scored a disputed run on an infield hit by Roger Repoz. He was originally ruled out on interference, and that would have been the third out, but the call was overturned, allowing the go-ahead run to score. Sam Mele lodged a protest, and the league president would have to rule on the call if the Twins lost the game. In the last of the ninth the Twins got Rich Rollins on board with one out, but then right-hander Pete Mikkelsen retired Oliva for the second out. That brought up Killebrew. Harmon worked the count full, then fouled off a change-up to stay alive. On the next pitch he connected, sending a two-run homer into the left-field seats to win the game.

Ten years later major-league baseball did a poll on the greatest moments in each team's history. Minnesota fans voted that home run by Harmon as the peak moment in Twins history.

The All-Star Game was played at Met Stadium that year. Everyone had been excited about it, although nobody had guessed that the Twins would be in first place at the time it was played. The Twins also had six players in the game: Oliva, Killebrew, Battey, Versalles, Grant, and Hall. I had the privilege of broadcasting the All-Star Game, along with Bob Prince, the longtime voice of the Pittsburgh Pirates.

It was quite a game. Milt Pappas of Baltimore started for the American League, and Willie Mays of the Giants hit his second pitch of the game for a home run. The National League built an early 5-0 lead, but the American League came back and finally tied the game in the fifth on a two-run homer by Killebrew. The National League still went on to win the game, but it was a real thriller.

It was fun working with Bob Prince, known for his occasional enjoyment of liquid refreshment, as in the following story. On a team flight to San Francisco, back when hard liquor was not allowed on team charter flights, Bob Prince carried a flask with him anyway. Joe Brown, the Pirates' general manager, noticed Prince drinking from his flask. Joe reminded him of the rule against liquor on the charter flights. Prince solemnly pulled out a doctor's letter prescribing so much Crown Royal a day for medicinal purposes. "Be that as it may," Brown said, "I think you better put that flask away for the rest of the trip." Bob complied.

After the All-Star break the Twins started having injury problems. They battled through a lot of injuries in 1965. Pascual was out for six weeks with a torn muscle in his back. Earl Battey, one of the top catchers in baseball, missed a few weeks with assorted injuries. Tony Oliva had a bone chip in his knuckle, but he still won the American League batting title for the second season in a row, becoming the first player to win the batting championship his first two full years in the big leagues. The bone chip created throwing problems, and when he took a full swing, Tony often lost his grip, and the bat would go flying off, sometimes into the box seats behind the Twins' dugout. And the real leader of the team, Harmon Killebrew, was out for seven weeks with a dislocated left elbow. That year Killebrew had moved from the outfield to first base and, in a play at first, had a collision with Baltimore's Russ Snyder, one of the speediest runners in the league. In the collision Snyder hooked and dislocated Harmon's left elbow. As a result of the injury, Harmon finished with only 25 home runs, his first season with fewer than 45 home runs since the Twins had come to Minnesota in 1961.

Despite the injuries, the Twins stayed hot. After the All-Star break they won nine out of eleven games in a home stand, taking a healthy lead. But the other teams kept battling. The White Sox had pulled to within five games in September, just before a two-game series at Comiskey Park.

In the first game the White Sox had a 2-1 lead in the seventh, when Jimmie Hall hit a two-run homer, his first since the one that had beaten Baltimore at the Met five weeks before. The Twins won 3-2, and took a six-game lead. They won again the next night and then won another five in a row. By Saturday, September 25, the Twins magic number was three: any combination of wins by the Twins or losses by their nearest competitor totalling three would clinch the pennant. In the first game of a doubleheader against the Senators at RFK Stadium, Mudcat Grant pitched a one-hitter and won his 20th game. The second game was tied in the eighth, when Quilici singled in two runs for a 5-3 lead. That was the final score, and the Twins' magic number was now one. The next day in Washington Jim Kaat went the distance and struck out Don Zimmer to end the game with a Twins' win, 2-1, clinching the pennant and setting off a wild celebration. The Twins had finished the regular season with 102 wins, still a team record.

Unfortunately for me, I was in Oakland announcing a Raiders game for NBC Television. Calvin Griffith also missed the game, since he was avoiding the District of Columbia because of a pending lawsuit from one of the Twins minority stockholders, Gabe Murphy. Calvin was at a Vikings game in Met Stadium and had watched the Twins on a television in the press box.

We still didn't know who would play against the Twins in

the World Series. For a while the San Francisco Giants looked likely, but the Giants' archrival, the Los Angeles Dodgers, finally pulled out the National League pennant, winning 15 of their last 16 games to finish two games ahead of San Francisco. The Dodgers, unlike the Twins, didn't have a powerful hitting lineup—they hit only 78 home runs that season. Instead, the Dodgers relied mostly on speed, fielding, and pitching. But what pitching it was, led by southpaw Sandy Koufax and big right-hander Don Drysdale. Koufax led the National League with 26 wins and an earned-run average just barely over two runs per game. Drysdale had won 23 games, and Claude Osteen, even though his record was 15-15, had an ERA under three. Although Koufax was the ace of the staff, he didn't open the World Series because he was Jewish and the first game fell on Yom Kippur. Drysdale started instead, and he was no slouch, but neither was the Twins' starter, Mudcat Grant.

The first two games of the World Series would be at Met Stadium, the next three at Dodger Stadium, and the rest, if necessary, back at the Met. Dodger Stadium in Los Angeles was set up to take advantage of their team's style of offense. They kept the infield rock-hard to help their speedy runners, and they allowed the grass along the foul lines to grow a little higher to help bunted balls stay fair. The Twins decided to counter that strategy with some creative groundskeeping at Met Stadium. To slow down the Dodger speedsters, they put a lot of extra dirt on the infield, so much that the umpires ordered them to remove some during the second game. Dick Ericson, the groundskeeper at the Met, says that they hauled off a couple of wheelbarrow loads but left a lot of extra dirt on the base paths.

In the series opener, at Met Stadium, Ron Fairly gave the Dodgers the lead with a home run in the top of the second. But in the bottom of that inning Don Mincher tied it with a home run in his first World Series at-bat. In the third the Twins scored six runs, the most runs the Dodgers had given up in a single inning during the entire season: Zoilo Versalles hit a three-run homer, and Frank Quilici had two hits, tying a World Series record for hits in an inning. Mudcat went the distance, and the Twins won the first game, 8-2.

The Twins faced Koufax in the second game, and, like everyone else that year, weren't able to do much. But they were able to scratch out a couple of runs, one of them unearned, off Koufax (and added three more off Ron Perranoski after Koufax had been removed for a pinch-hitter). That was more than enough for Jim Kaat, who allowed just one run while striking out nine in going the distance on a seven-hitter. This game is better remembered because of a great sliding catch Bob Allison made on a drive down the left-field line hit by Jim Lefebvre. The game was scoreless in the fifth, and the Dodgers had a runner on base at the time. It could have been real trouble for the Twins had Bob not made that catch. The Twins won the game, 5-1, taking a 2-0 lead, and the series shifted to Los Angeles.

In the third game Claude Osteen, perhaps the best number-three pitcher in baseball that year, pitched against Camilo Pascual, who was still feeling the effects of his mid-season back surgery. Osteen shut out the Twins, 4-0, in a brisk game lasting just two hours and six minutes.

In the fourth game Killebrew and Oliva hit homers, but Drysdale struck out 11 and twirled a five-hitter. Mudcat wasn't nearly as sharp as he had been in the first game, allowing four earned runs in five innings. Los Angeles won, 7-2, and the teams were tied.

The fifth game was no contest. The Dodgers scored twice off Kaat in the first inning and went on to a 7-0 win. Koufax pitched a four-hit shutout, striking out ten.

The Twins' total for the three games in Los Angeles was

two runs and 14 hits in 27 innings. But although they were now down, 3-2, in the series, the Twins still felt they had a chance, considering how well they had played in the first two games at the Met. But their backs were to the wall: they would have to win two in a row to take the series.

In the sixth game, with Mudcat Grant facing Claude Osteen, they looked liked their old selves when Bob Allison gave the Twins a 2-0 lead with a home run in the fourth. Then Mudcat parked one of the reliever Howie Reed's pitches in the left-field seats, a three-run homer that gave the Twins a 5-0 lead. Mudcat later told me that he was still looking where the ball had landed as he rounded second, and he missed the base. The Dodgers didn't notice, but had they appealed, Grant would have been credited only with a single, although two of the runs would still have scored. I asked Mudcat why he hadn't gone back and touched second base. "Well, I didn't think the Dodgers had noticed," he told me, "and then I realized there were nearly 50,000 people in the stands and we were on national television, so I would have been kind of embarrassed to go back and touch second in front of all those people."

The series came down to the seventh game. Jim Kaat would start for the Twins on two days' rest. He had pitched only two and a third innings the fifth game, so he was in relatively good shape. Dodger manager Walter Alston didn't have the same luxury with his starters, all of whom had pitched complete games in Los Angeles. It was Drysdale's turn in the rotation, but Alston decided to go with Koufax, even though Sandy had worked nine innings just three days before. It would be a classic matchup as one game would determine the world champions.

The game was scoreless into the fourth, when Dodger left-fielder Lou Johnson pulled a long fly down the line and off the left-field foul pole for a home run. The Dodgers added a second run in that inning on a single by first base-man Wes Parker, one of the Dodgers' four switch-hitting in-fielders (along with Jim Gilliam, Maury Wills, and Jim Lefebvre). Now the Twins were down, 2-0. In the last of the fifth they had runners on first and second, with one out. Zoilo Versalles drilled one down the third-base line. It looked like a sure double that would score at least one run, maybe two, but Gilliam made a great diving stop, scram-bled to his feet, and ran to third for a force out. Gilliam had been playing right on the line, not where a third baseman usually would be positioned. Then Nossek forced Versalles at second, ending the inning. That was the last gasp for the Twins. Koufax set them down in order in the sixth through the eighth but then gave up a one-out single to Killebrew with one out in the ninth. The tying runs came to the plate, but Koufax struck out Battey and Allison to end it. It was a great performance by Koufax: a three-hit shutout and ten strikeouts on just two days' rest. Koufax and Drysdale had pitched five of the seven games.

Disappointed as the Twins fans were, they were proud of their team. The Twins later played in two more World Series and won both of them, but many old-timers, myself in-cluded, are still talking about 1965.

Jim Kaat is still the only Twins pitcher to win 25 games in a season. *WCCO Radio.*

Near Miss

The Twins got off to a horrible start in 1966. On the Fourth of July they were eight games under .500 with 35 wins and 43 losses. They posted a 54-30 record the rest of the way but never overcame their slow start. They finished second, a distant second, nine games behind the mighty Orioles, who won 97 games in the regular season and then shocked the Dodgers with a four-game sweep in the World Series.

Jim Kaat won 25 games that year, and he's still the only Twins 25-game winner. With that kind of a season, you might think he'd win the Cy Young Award, but until 1967 only one Cy Young was awarded for both leagues, and for the second-straight season the honor went to Sandy Koufax of the Dodgers in the National League. Otherwise, it's likely Kitty would have received a Cy Young Award for 1966. (For that matter, had there been separate awards in 1965 there's a good chance Mudcat Grant could have won the Cy Young Award although Mel Stottlemyre of the Yankees or Sam Mc-Dowell of the Indians would have been contenders for it, as well.)

The Twins offense bogged down, but it still exploded from time to time. In a game against the Kansas City Athletics at the Met in June, the Twins hit five home runs—the last three in succession—in one inning. Rich Rollins, Zoilo Versalles, Tony Oliva, Don Mincher, and, as usual, Harmon Killebrew supplied the power. Harmon finished second in the American League with 39 homers and 110 RBIs, and Tony Oliva was second in batting average at .307.

Frank Robinson of the Orioles was tops in batting average, home runs, and RBIs, in addition to a couple of other offensive departments. He won the American League Triple Crown and received the league's Most Valuable Player Award. Robinson, playing his first year in the American League, and was certainly the most important factor in Baltimore's success that year. The Orioles had traded Milt Pappas to get Robinson from Cincinnati, where five years earlier he had been named the National League's Most Valuable Player. He's still the only player ever named MVP in both leagues.

I remember 1966 for another reason: an incident off the field in July. Many airlines were on strike that year, and major-league baseball temporarily rescinded the rule that had prohibited two teams from flying on the same plane. After finishing a series in Minnesota, the Twins and Yankees were on the same flight to Washington, where the Twins would be playing, while the Yankees were flying home to New York. The chartered flight was delayed by more than three hours, and many of the Yankees whiled away the time at the airport bar.

When they boarded the plane, Mickey Mantle, Roger Maris, Joe Pepitone, and Hal Reniff were making a lot of noise. The flight crew was having trouble getting them seated and announced that the captain would not take off until everyone was buckled in. Reniff and Pepitone said they might just give the pilot a going over if he didn't take off. Billy Martin, one of the Twins' coaches, was a former Yankee and a drinking buddy of Mantle's, so Howard Fox, the Twins' traveling secretary, said, "Billy, why don't you make your Yankee friends behave?" As a Twins' coach, Billy figured that the Yankees' behavior problems should be handled by their manager, Ralph Houk. Houk, an ex-Marine and a veteran of the Battle of the Bulge, eventually settled his players down by grabbing Reniff and threatening to punch him.

That wasn't the end of it. From Dulles Airport we had a long bus ride to our hotel, the Washington Hilton. Billy Martin was sitting up front, across from Howard Fox and his wife. Sitting near the back of the bus, I heard Billy taunting Fox for asking him to settle down the Yankees. At the hotel Fox picked up all the room keys and handed them out as usual. He gave Martin his key last. I'm told that Howard flipped the key to Billy, who muttered, "One of these days you're going to get decked." Fox challenged Billy to follow up on his threat right then, and Billy popped him in the jaw. Allison was still in the lobby, and he grabbed Billy to stop the fracas. But that wasn't the end of the stormy relationship between Fox and Martin, and, of course, it wasn't the last explosive incident involving Billy Martin.

Around this time there was a funny incident involving Martin. He was assigned the job of making sure the players were in by a certain time when the team was on the road. He'd usually call all the rooms around 1 a.m. Once, Kathy was with me on a road trip, and there was a mixup with the rooms at the Roosevelt Hotel in New York. Kathy and I ended up with the room that Jim Kaat and Shorty Pleis were supposed to get. When Billy called, thinking he was checking up on Kaat and Pleis, Kathy answered the phone. Kitty and Shorty were about the last guys in the world who would have a woman in their room, so you can imagine Billy's surprise when he heard a female voice.

Everything considered, 1966 was a year the Twins wanted to forget. For 1967 they made some changes, of which the most important was the acquisition of Dean Chance from the Angels. Chance had won the Cy Young Award in 1964, quite a feat since he was pitching for an expansion team that wasn't very good. For Chance the Twins gave up two key members of their pennant-winning team, Don Mincher and Jimmie Hall. Although Mincher still had a few good seasons left in him, Jimmie's best years were behind him. In 1963 Jimmie had broken in with the Twins with 33 home runs, but the next year he was beaned by Bo Belinsky, a southpaw with the Angels, and he was never the same after that. He was a left-handed batter and yet was hit on the left side of his face. He turned around so far away from a high inside pitch that the ball fractured his left cheekbone. Afterward he was still an effective hitter against right-handed pitchers, but against a good left-hander he often bailed out. In 1967 Chance won 20 games and joined Jim Kaat and Dave Boswell in topping 200 strikeouts, the only time the Twins have had three pitchers with more than 200 strikeouts in the same season.

Another off-season change involving the pitching was the release of Johnny Sain as pitching coach. Kaat sent the Twin Cities newspapers an open letter asking that they keep Sain and hire a manager who could "take advantage of Sain's talents." Sain was hired by the Tigers, and the Twins' new pitching coach was Early Wynn, who had saved Calvin Griffith from being thrown over a railroad bridge nearly 30 years before.

In addition to the changes on the field, Ray Scott, one of the Twins' original announcers, resigned and was replaced by Merle Harmon. Merle never missed a chance to soak in some rays, and once before the game on a bright sunny day in Milwaukee he sat in the bleachers with his shirt off. Our broadcast crew still operated the same way: with televised games one of us announced for television and the other for radio, and with games on the radio only we announced in shifts, while Halsey, as the color man, was in the radio booth the entire game.

In 1967 the Twins got off to another slow start with too many mental mistakes, as though they just weren't ready to play. After one exasperating loss early in the season Sam Mele ordered the team to stay after the game and work out. A couple of days later in a game at Detroit Tovar was on first when Oliva hit a high drive to right off Denny McLain. Tiger outfielder Al Kaline drifted back for it, and Tovar, assuming the ball would be caught, started back toward first, instead of remaining halfway down the line toward second. Well, the ball wasn't caught. It went into the seats for a home run—or what should have been a home run. Instead, as Oliva ran to first, he was watching Kaline and the ball. As he rounded first, Oliva passed Tovar and was called out. Instead of a two-run homer, Oliva was credited with only a single. Later in that game after a wild pitch Jim Ollom left home plate uncovered, allowing Ray Oyler to score all the way from second.

The problems reached a peak on June 8 when the Twins gave up four runs to Cleveland in the top of the ninth and lost, bringing their record to 25-25. The next day Griffith fired Mele. The new manager was Cal Ermer, who had long been associated with the Griffith organization, although he had also spent some time as a coach with the Orioles. Most recently, Ermer had managed the Twins' top farm team in Denver, and in the minors he had managed 11 of the current Twins, including Allison and Killebrew at Chattanooga in 1957.

The Twins didn't catch fire immediately under Ermer, playing .500 ball for the first couple weeks, but then they took off. What developed was a great four-team race, possibly the greatest pennant races in the history of the American League. The Chicago White Sox and the Detroit Tigers, the early front-runners, were now joined by the Twins. The fourth team was the Boston Red Sox, who hadn't won a pennant in 21 years and who had finished ninth the year before.

One game soon after Ermer became manager was unusually exciting. On June 18 in Cleveland in a pitcher's duel that lasted until the eighth inning, Tony Oliva, just out of the hospital for some minor problems, came off the bench to pinch hit with the bases loaded. He stroked a double and put the Twins up by three runs. But the Indians loaded the bases with two out in the bottom of the inning, and shortstop Larry Brown hit a long fly to left. It looked like a grand slam that would put Cleveland ahead. But the wind held the ball up just a little, and Sandy Valdespino, who had just entered the game as a defensive replacement, raced back, grabbed the top of the fence and pulled himself up—he was only five foot seven, but he really got up there—and snared the ball.

In late June and early July the Twins won eight in a row and had pulled within two and a half games of the first-place White Sox, as they opened a four-game series in Chicago. In the series opener Dean Chance, who had won 11 in a row, carried a 1-0 lead into the last of the ninth, when the White Sox loaded the bases with one out. Al Worthington, who had an outstanding year in 1967, relieved Chance. Don Buford popped out, and Ron Hansen hit a grounder to Versalles at short. It looked as though the game was over. But the ball bounced off the heel of Zoilo's glove into center field, and two runs scored. Because of this error, the Twins lost, 2-1, and they were now three and a half games out. They lost another heartbreaker again the next day, but did manage to sweep a doubleheader to salvage a series split and pull back to just two-and-a-half out (right where they had been when the series started) as they went into the All-Star break.

In August at the Met in a three-game series with the Red Sox, the Twins won the first two. In the third, on Sunday, August 6, Chance went up against Jim Lonborg, who was having a great year. Because of rain, the game was called in the last of the fifth inning, just barely long enough to be an official game. Chance had retired all 15 batters. It was a five-inning perfect game, the first no-hitter Chance pitched as a professional, although he had pitched 18 no-hitters in high school at Wooster, Ohio. The Twins won the game, 2-0, and moved past Boston into second place, still two and a half games behind the White Sox.

On August 13 the Twins moved into the top spot for the first time all season, after a three-game sweep of the Chicago White Sox. From then on, they were never more than a game and a half out of first place and never more than two games in front.

Near the end of August, in the second game of a double-header at Cleveland, Chance walked the first two batters. Early Wynn came out to the mound for a chat, and Dean settled down, although he still allowed a run that inning because of an error and a wild pitch. The Twins tied it up in the second and took the lead in the sixth. Meanwhile, Chance was cruising. Despite the run he had given up in the first, he hadn't allowed a hit, and he carried the no-hitter into the ninth inning. He finished it off by getting Tony Horton to ground out. Less than three weeks before, he had pitched a rain-shortened perfect game. Now he had a full nine-inning no-hitter. It the Twins' first nine-inning no-hitter since Kralick's in 1962, and it was their last for 27 years. And Chance's gem put the Twins back in first place, half a game ahead of Chicago and Boston.

Chance even survived a beanball duel in this game. After Cleveland starter Sonny Siebert knocked down Killebrew with a pitch in the fourth, Chance retaliated with a high inside pitch to Tony Horton. Dino was never averse to dusting a guy off if he thought the opposing pitcher had thrown at one of his hitters. The next time Chance came to the plate, Siebert drilled him with a fastball. On his way to first Chance had some words for Siebert, who started toward him, but several players rushed between them.

The pennant race went right down to the wire. The White Sox, who had set the pace most of the season, dropped out, but the Twins, Red Sox, and Tigers were all going strong into the final weekend of the season. The Twins were in first place by one game over both Boston and Detroit. The Twins would finish the season with games on Saturday and Sunday at Boston, while Detroit was finishing up at home with back-to-back doubleheaders against California. Just one win by the Twins would finish off the Red Sox and clinch at least a tie with Detroit, unless the Tigers could pull off a pair of sweeps against the Angels.

For the first game at Boston Jim Kaat was on a roll. He had won seven straight games and had struck out 13 in his last outing. He started off fine against the Red Sox, but in the third inning as he delivered a pitch, something popped in his elbow, and he had to leave the game. Jim Perry relieved him and held the Red Sox scoreless for two more innings, and the Twins carried a 2-0 lead into the last of the sixth. But then the Red Sox broke through with a couple of runs to tie it. Then George Scott greeted reliever Ron Kline with a home run on the first pitch of the seventh inning to put the Red Sox ahead. Yastrzemski and then Killebrew later homered in the game, in effect canceling each other out, and the Red Sox won, 6-4, to pull into a first-place tie. Meanwhile, the Tigers split their doubleheader with the Angels and were a half-game back of the leaders.

The Twins' final game of the season featured a great matchup between Dean Chance and Jim Lonborg. Again the

Twins carried a 2-0 lead into the sixth inning. Again the Red Sox rallied in the sixth. Yastrzemski hit a two-run single, tying the game, and, with some sloppy fielding by the Twins, the Sox scored three more runs and won, 5-3. They then huddled around a radio in their clubhouse to find out what was happening in Detroit. When the Tigers lost the second game of their doubleheader, the Red Sox became the American League champions.

Although the Twins came up short, Harmon Killebrew had another great year, banging 44 home runs, tying for the lead league with Boston's Carl Yastrzemski. He also hit a pair of the longest home runs I've ever seen in back-to-back games. In a game against California at the Met on June 3, Harmon's homer off Lew Burdette landed in the second deck of the seats in left field, the longest home run in the history of the Met. A shopping center now stands on the site of Met Stadium, and the mall owners placed a marker at the site of home plate and put up a seat on a wall where Killebrew's home run supposedly landed, although in relation to the home plate-marker the seat doesn't appear to be in the correct location. The next day Harmon's homer hit the facing of the upper deck. It was a rising line drive, and although it didn't reach the upper deck, it might have been hit harder. Harmon hit this one off Jack Sanford, who roomed with Lew Burdette, who had given up the other shot. After the game Sanford said, "I got the book on how to pitch to Killebrew from my roommate."

Another outstanding player for the Twins that year was Cesar Tovar, who overcame his early blunders to become one of the best lead-off hitters in the league. Carl Yastrzemski was not a unanimous choice as the league's Most Valuable Player because Tovar received a first-place vote from Max Nichols, a sportswriter for the *Minneapolis Star*. Nichols angered a lot of people around the country by voting for

Tovar, but Cesar had quite a season, playing six different defensive positions and providing a real spark on offense. Yastrzemski was the overwhelming pick for MVP. Not only did he win the American League Triple Crown, he carried the Red Sox after Boston's fine young outfielder Tony Conigliaro was beaned and seriously hurt.

For the Red Sox, in achieving their "Impossible Dream," their win over the Twins in the 1967 season finale remains one of the most memorable games in Boston baseball history. For the Twins this game remains one of their most heartbreaking losses ever.

Rising in the West

The Twins had high hopes in 1968, especially after winning their first seven games of the season. Then everything went downhill. They were hampered by the loss of Kaat for the first part of the season. That pop in his elbow in his last start of the 1967 season turned out to be a torn muscle. It took more than the off-season to heal: he was out for the first five weeks of the 1968 season. Even after he returned, the Twins had a slump in the second half of the season and finished 1968 in seventh place. This was known as the Year of the Pitcher. There was only one .300 hitter in the American League, Carl Yastrzemski, and he barely made it, finishing at .301. Meanwhile, the Tigers' Denny McLain won 31 games, and Bob Gibson in the National League had an ERA of 1.12.

The Twins got a first-hand look at the Year of the Pitcher on May 8 in a twilight game at Oakland. Jim "Catfish" Hunter, the A's right-hander, pitched the first regular-season perfect game in the American League in 46 years. And Hunter had three hits in the game himself. With the Twins' last batter, pinch-hitter Rich Reese, Catfish fell behind in the count, two balls and one strike. Then Reese fouled off four pitches, just barely staying alive. Catfish missed with his next pitch, and the count was full. Hunter fired a fastball, and Reese swung and missed, ending the game. Catfish had his perfect game. Halsey later said that plate umpire Jerry Neudecker had done the best job of calling balls and strikes he had ever seen. Keep in mind he was saying this about a game the Twins had lost, which just goes to show you what a fair-minded announcer Halsey was.

Even after that disappointing season, the Twins were optimistic going into 1969, the first year of division play. The majors had added four new teams, in Seattle, Kansas City, Montreal, and San Diego, creating a total of 24 teams, 12 in each league, and had split the American League and National League into the Western and Eastern divisions of six teams each. In the new American League Western Division, in which the Twins would be a member, there would be only one team that had finished ahead of them the previous year; that was the Oakland Athletics (the A's had moved to Oakland from Kansas City after the 1967 season). Also in the West were the California Angels and Chicago White Sox, who had finished in a tie for eighth place in 1968, eight games behind the Twins. And both of the new expansion teams, the Seattle Pilots and Kansas City Royals, were in the Western Division.

Another reason for excitement among Twins fans was that the team had a new manager, Billy Martin. Martin played for the Twins and had been a coach on the team when it won the pennant. He had since gone down to the minors to manage. When manager Cal Ermer was fired after the 1968 season, Billy was hired.

Cal Ermer was a solid baseball man and an easygoing guy, usually. He could become riled by losing or by an umpire's call. He was a former soccer player and when he lost an argument with an umpire, he'd tear off his hat, throw it on the ground, and kick it soccer-style. He told me that when he was managing at Chattanooga, he once went into his soccer routine and kicked his hat—and also kicked umpire Lee Weyer in the shins. Of course, he was thrown out of the game and suspended and fined. But usually Ermer didn't show his emotions. In 1968, with Martin managing in Denver, Ermer felt there was an ax hanging over his head. A couple times during that season he asked me if I'd heard anything about Griffith's plans for the next year. "I'd sure like to have another shot at it," he'd say. Apparently Griffith thought Ermer had insufficient control of the ballclub so he hired fiery disciplinarian Billy Martin.

The season opener was in Kansas City against the brand-new Royals, who won their first two games against the Twins, both in extra innings, the first one 12 innings and the second one 17. The Twins went to California and lost two more games before their first win of the year, the first of a seven-game winning streak. From California they went to Seattle and beat the Pilots and then came home and beat the Angels with a shutout by left-hander Tommy Hall, a pitcher so lithe he was nicknamed the Blade. Also that April, at Comiskey Park in Chicago, Harmon Killebrew hit the 400th home run of his career, off Gary Peters.

In mid-May the Baltimore Orioles, considered one of the top contenders for the American League East title along with the defending world-champion Detroit Tigers, came to the Met for a series. In the opener the Orioles had a 2-1 lead in the last of the eighth. Baltimore southpaw Mike Cuellar, who would go on to tie for the Cy Young Award, was in control until Rod Carew, with a runner on board, hit an inside-the-park home run off him. The Twins won the game, 4-2.

Carew was now in his third season in the majors. He had won the American League Rookie of the Year Award when he broke in with the Twins in 1967. In 1969, he won the American League batting title with an average of .332. The biggest question in the batting race was whether Rod would have enough plate appearances to qualify for the batting crown, since he was often gone on military duty, which included several weekends and two weeks of summer camp. He ended up with 504 plate appearances, only two more than the minimum. Carew went on to a tremendous career in the majors, winning a total of seven batting titles with the Twins before finishing his career with the California Angels. He had a career total of more than 3,000 hits and was elected to the Hall of Fame in his first year of eligibility.

At first Rod was hard to get to know and was somewhat immature. In his first or second year he got really down once. We were on the road, I think in Cleveland, and he packed up and left for the airport to go home. Cal Ermer, the manager then, sent Johnny Goryl to talk him into staying. Rod matured greatly over the years, and we became good friends. After he was elected to the Hall of Fame in 1991, he asked me to introduce him at the induction ceremonies in Cooperstown, but as it turned out, the Commissioner of Baseball always gives the introduction.

Rod has always been fond of our daughter, Terri. When Terri was five, a spring-training game was rained out at Tinker Field in Orlando. Terri amused herself making mudpies on the hood of a car in the player's lot. It was Rod's car. "What are you doing?" he said to Terri when he discovered what she was doing. "Don't you know this is my car? Are these mudpies?" Terri nodded. Rod said, "All right, I'll tell you what. From now on your name is Mudpie." And to this day he still calls her Mudpie.

Even though he won the batting title in 1969, Carew overshadowed that performance with his exciting baserunning. He had 19 stolen bases, and seven were of home plate, breaking Ty Cobb's American League record and tying Pete Reiser's major-league record.

Cesar Tovar set a team record with 45 stolen bases and also did a fine job at the plate. The Orioles found him especially pesky. Two nights after Carew had beaten Cuellar with the inside-the-park home run, the Orioles' Dave Mc-Nally beat the Twins in a 5-0 shutout, but he lost his chance at a no-hitter when Tovar singled in the ninth for the Twins' only hit of the game. Later in the season, in the ninth inning of a game at Baltimore, Tovar singled to break up Mike Cuellar's no-hit bid.

McNally's next outing at the Met after the missed no-hitter was even more frustrating for him. It was on the first weekend in August, Campers' Weekend, an annual Twins' function that always brought in huge crowds, and for this series the Twins had crowds over 40,000 for each game. The series finale, on Sunday, August 3, featured a great pitching matchup between left-handers Kaat and McNally, who had a season record of 15-0 coming into the game and was on the verge of tying or setting league records for consecutive victories in one season, over two seasons, and at the start of a season. In the top of the first Frank Robinson of the Orioles was ejected for his behavior after striking out, and when Earl Weaver, the manager, came out to argue, he got the thumb, too. In the last of the first the Twins had a two-out rally when Killebrew doubled and Oliva singled, but Harmon was thrown out at the plate by center-fielder Paul Blair, ending the inning. That was the closest the Twins came to scoring off McNally for a while. The Orioles scratched out a run in the fourth, and McNally held that 1-0 margin into the seventh, when he retired Oliva and Allison on flies to center field. But then Leo Cardenas and Frank Quilici each singled, and the crowd started to stir. Tom Tischinski, a light-hitting catcher, was due up next, but Martin sent up Rick Renick to hit for him. Renick worked McNally for a walk, and the bases were loaded.

Kaat was the next scheduled hitter, but Billy sent in left-handed hitting Rich Reese, who would finish the 1969 season with a .322 batting average. However, he usually was platooned, and most of his at-bats were against right-handers. Now against the southpaw McNally, Reese worked the count, which seesawed back and forth until it was full. Reese fouled the next pitch off and then lifted a fly ball that started to carry. Left-fielder Don Buford went back on it, looking like he might have a chance to catch it, but the ball kept drifting and came down in the left-field seats for a grand-slam home run. I don't think I ever heard a crowd make so much noise as they did on that home run. The Twins ended up winning the game, 5-2, to tag McNally with his first loss of the season. Despite that, the Orioles dominated the season series with the Twins.

Oakland was the Twins' biggest rival for the Western Division title. Oakland outfielder Reggie Jackson was on a home-run binge over the first half of the season. He had 33 home runs going into a three-game series that began on Friday, July 4, in Minnesota. On Saturday in the first inning of the second game of the series Jackson hit one of the longest home runs I've ever seen by a left-handed batter. Reggie boomed a pitch from Jim Perry off the top of the scoreboard in right-center field, hitting at the far left side of the scoreboard toward center field. It's estimated the ball would have traveled 515 feet unimpeded, and if it had cleared the scoreboard, it would have been the only ball ever hit out of Met Stadium. Surprisingly, Jackson hit only 13 more home runs that season and was surpassed by both Killebrew and Washington's Frank Howard.

Killebrew's performance in that series shows how much the team relied on him. Oakland led the Twins by a game as the series started. In the series opener, a morning game on Independence Day, Killebrew roughed up Catfish Hunter early with his 20th homer of the season to cap a three-run first. The Twins won the game, 10-4. The next day, in the top of the first inning the A's took the early lead on Jackson's monster home run off the scoreboard, but Harmon wiped that out with a two-run homer in the last of the first, and in the second inning he hit another homer with two on base. In that game he had six RBIs as Perry won his seventh game, 13-1. In the final game of the series Oakland had a 6-2 lead, but the Twins rallied in the last of the seventh. Three runs were in and a runner was on first as Killebrew stepped in against Roland Fingers, who went on to a Hall of Fame career as one of the best relief pitchers ever. A stiff wind blowing in from left field, but it wasn't enough to keep Harmon from crunching a two-run homer to put the Twins ahead to stay.

That gave Killebrew 82 RBIs in the Twins' first 80 games. He now had 23 home runs, still far behind Jackson, but eventually he passed Jackson and finished the year with 49 home runs, tying his own team record. He also set a team mark with 140 runs batted in. He was named the American League Most Valuable Player, the second Twin to receive this honor, after Versalles in 1965.

The Twins had a big four-game series with the A's in Oakland in September. The Athletics, trailing the Twins by six and a half games, needed to win at least three to stay in the race. Instead, the Twins took three out of four. In the opener Tovar hit a grand slam in the tenth inning to win it for the Twins. The A's won the second game. The third game went all the way to the 18th inning, and then Tovar hit a two-run homer to win it. In the fourth game Killebrew hit a three-run homer and then a grand slam for seven RBIs in a 16-4 win.

In 1969 Dave Boswell and Jim Perry each won 20 games for the first time in his career. Perry's victory over Oakland on July 5 was only his seventh win of the year, but on September 20 he won his 20th, beating the Pilots, 3-2, as Oliva doubled Carew home from first in the last of the ninth.

The Twins had the chance to clinch the division at home

the next afternoon, but even though Harmon hit two homers, the Pilots won when John Kennedy broke a 3-3 tie with a home run in the top of the ninth. The clincher came the next night, in Kansas City, where the Twins had started the season with two losses. The Twins finished the regular season with 97 wins and led the entire league with 710 runs. For the first time in his career Tony Oliva topped 100 runs batted in. The Twins had an excellent bullpen: Al Worthington was joined by Ron Perranoski. Leo Cardenas played great at shortstop, and Rich Reese had an outstanding year playing part-time.

In the clubhouse after the game that clinched the division crown, the guys were whooping it up when one of the writers asked Killebrew how it felt to be the Western Division champions. "Well, it feels pretty good," Harmon said, "but, you know, we really haven't won anything yet. We've won our division, but to win the pennant, we've still got to beat the Eastern Division team, and that means we're going to have to beat Baltimore in the American League playoffs."

The American League playoffs, the first ever held, opened in Baltimore. At that time the playoffs were a best-of-five series, and the first two games were scheduled in Baltimore and the remaining games in Minnesota. The first two games turned out to be classics.

In the first game, thanks to a two-run home by Oliva in the seventh, the Twins carried a 3-2 lead into the last of the ninth. But then Boog Powell led off the ninth with a home run off Jim Perry, tying the game. Perranoski relieved Perry later in the inning and stayed in the game into the last of the twelfth. The Orioles had Mark Belanger on third with two out when Paul Blair dropped a bunt softly down the third-base line. It rolled to a stop about halfway down the line, giving catcher John Roseboro and Killebrew, playing third, no chance of making a play. Belanger raced home for the winning run.

They had another heartbreaker the next day in a great pitching duel between McNally and Boswell, both 20-game winners. It was scoreless through ten innings, with both starters still on the hill. After surrendering three hits early on, McNally had not allowed a hit since the fourth, and in the eleventh he put the Twins down again without any trouble. Boswell, although he had walked seven in the game, was pitching nearly as well, but Boog Powell got aboard and advanced to second with two out. At this point Perranoski, a southpaw, came in for Boswell. Earl Weaver countered by sending up right-handed Curt Motton as a pinch hitter, and Motton singled Powell home for the win, giving the Orioles a 2-0 lead in the series. The Twins now faced the Herculean task of having to win three in a row from a team that had lost only 53 of 162 games during the regular season.

For the third game the Orioles went with Jim Palmer. He had been on the disabled list part of the 1969 season, but he had still finished with an outstanding record of 16-4, including a no-hitter. Martin was expected to start Jim Kaat, who had a 14-13 record that year, but Billy surprised everybody, including Cal Griffith, by going with right-hander Bob Miller, who had alternated between starting and relieving that year. Miller had started only 11 games and should not have started this one. He lasted less than two innings, and the Orioles romped to an 11-2 victory and the pennant.

Oliva, with five hits in 13 at-bats, including a home run, was the only Twin to hit over .300 in the series. His arm was bothering him a great deal, and in the final game, at Met Stadium, he even made an underhanded throw back to infield. The frustrated fans, not understanding that Tony was hurt, booed him, in one of the few times I've heard anyone boo Oliva.

This was the end for Billy Martin with the Twins, after

only one season as manager. A lot of incidents did not sit well with the home office.

The most notable was the fight between Billy and Dave Boswell in August at the Lindell AC, a nightclub near the hotel in Detroit. Martin was with pitching coach Art Fowler, who was complaining that Boswell had refused to do his required running that afternoon. Fowler, unlike Johnny Sain, believed in having his pitchers run between starts. Fowler was Billy's drinking buddy and a good pitching coach on the many teams Martin managed in the future. When Dave Boswell came into the bar, Billy confronted him about not having done his running. The conversation became heated, and Bob Allison tried to intercede, but Billy rushed Boswell with a series of punches. Even though he was battered black and blue, Boswell joked about the incident, but no one was laughing back in the Twins' offices in Minnesota.

There was another incident when the Twins were to play an exhibition game against their top farm team in Toledo. A couple of the regulars asked Billy if they could be excused from playing in the game. Billy asked Griffith if that would be okay, and Calvin refused because he had assured the people in Toledo that all the players would be there. Billy let two players off anyway. Calvin was not at all happy about that.

The final straw must have been when Billy started Bob Miller in the third game of the playoffs instead of Kaat. At the end of the season Griffith decided not to renew Billy's contract. Billy was enormously popular in Minnesota, and the fans were outraged. There were "Bring Billy Back" bumper stickers all over town, and a lot of fans vowed they would never go to another Twins game. Every so often in later years I heard from people who said they hadn't been back since Martin was fired.

As far as my relationship with Billy went, I found Billy

very accommodating when I needed information. Once he even offered to give me his signs so I could predict the plays, but I declined. I just preferred to call the game after the fact.

As many fans know, it seemed impossible for Billy to stay out of trouble. Shortly after he signed Billy as manager, Calvin said, "I feel like I'm sitting on a powder keg."

On a couple of occasions Billy even jumped on Halsey Hall, who was as likable a fellow as you could find anywhere. After Boswell lost a tough game, 2-1, even though he had pitched very well, as the players were coming out of the stadium and getting on the team bus, Halsey gave Boswell a slap on the back and said, "Too bad, Bozzie, you pitched a great game."

Billy Martin screamed at Halsey, "Don't you be telling my pitcher he pitched a great game when he lost!"

Another time, early in the season, Dick Woodson low-bridged Oakland's Reggie Jackson with two head-high fastballs after Jackson had hit two home runs earlier in the game. After the second beanball attempt, Jackson charged the mound. It turned into the usual wrestling match—nothing serious. Afterward, on a flight to Chicago for a series with the White Sox, I was talking about the incident with Halsey, who said, "Well, I suppose when you throw two pitches in a row at a guy's head, you can't blame him for charging the mound."

Billy Martin overheard and yelled, "Halsey, whose side are you on?"

That's a question a lot of us wondered about Billy. There's no question that he knew baseball. He was always looking for some way to get that extra edge on the other ball club. He believed in playing an aggressive running type of game, forcing the other team into making mistakes. Billy went on to manage several other clubs: the Tigers, Rangers, A's, and the Yankees on several occasions. He always seemed most successful in his first year with each team. One of the things that worked against continued success for him was his habit of getting into feuds with his own ballplayers. While managing the Yankees in 1977, for example, he got into a row with Reggie Jackson, who at this time was playing in New York. On national television, the two of them almost came to blows in the Yankee dugout during a game at Fenway Park.

Some say that Martin did better in his first year with a team because he overworked the pitching staff. Billy has denied that, but, for example, in 1971, his first year with the Detroit Tigers, he had Mickey Lolich pitch 376 innings, a tremendous total. When he took over at Oakland in 1980 with a good young staff consisting of Rick Langford, Matt Keough, Steve McCatty, and Mike Norris, Billy often left the starters in, even after they were tiring in the late innings. He got some good performances out of these pitchers for a couple of years, but they all ended up with bad arms. By that time, of course, Martin was elsewhere.

After firing Martin, Griffith was asked by CBS Radio what his plans were for naming a new manager. In true Calvin style, he answered, "I can't tell you exactly what I'm going to do, but I can tell you one thing, that it won't be anything rational." Calvin eventually hired Bill Rigney as manager. Rigney had been a player-manager with the Minneapolis Millers in the American Association in the 1950s. He then became manager of the New York Giants and then the first manager of the Los Angeles Angels. Since the decision to replace Martin was unpopular, Griffith mentioned to me before spring training that it was important for the Twins to get off to a good start in 1970, but the Twins won only seven and lost 20 games during spring training, just about their worst spring record ever. In the regular season they rebounded and won the Western Division by nine games, the same margin as in 1969, and they won 98 games, one more than the previous year with Martin.

In 1970 when Merle Harmon left the broadcast team, I had two new partners on radio and a new one on television. Ray Christensen was in line to work with me, but because of a on-the-air conflict the station temporarily assigned Al Shaver, an outstanding hockey announcer, as my radio partner for a few weeks into the season, until Ray Christensen could join me.

Ray has been the voice of the University of Minnesota Gopher football team since 1951 and has done play-by-play for Gopher basketball nearly as long. He worked with me on Twins games for four years. We changed the way we alternated between radio and television announcing. Ray did only radio, and Frank Buetel announced only the televised games. As in the past, Halsey and I moved back and forth between booths during the televised games. In the following season I was exclusively on radio.

The Twins had another good season in 1970, but about a third of the way through the season Rod Carew, playing at second base, was badly injured while turning a double play in Milwaukee. Mike Hegan of the Brewers came in with a rolling block. He collided with Carew and tore up Rod's knee. Carew, hitting .376 at the time, was out for most of the rest of the season. Frank Quilici filled in some at second, and Danny Thompson was called up from the minors to replace Carew. After Rod returned to second base, Thompson moved to shortstop. Danny didn't have a lot of power, but he made few mistakes and was a good solid day-in, day-out player. Danny kept playing even after he was diagnosed with leukemia a couple of years later. In 1976 the Twins traded him to the Texas Rangers, and at the end of that season Danny died. He was just 29.

Bert Blyleven joined the Twins in 1970, and in his first

game, in Washington, he gave up a home run to the first batter he faced, Lee Maye, but then he didn't allow another run
in the seven innings he pitched. He won the game, 2-1, and
ended up winning ten games for the Twins that year. Even
though he was only 19, Bert already had a great arm with a
very good fastball and an even better curveball. It was the
curve that was his trademark throughout his career until his
waning years, when he had arm trouble and resorted to off-
speed stuff. With a record of 10-9 in 1970, he didn't have a
great rookie season, and he never seemed to have much
support from his hitters. He lost a lot of low-scoring games,
but he finished his career with nearly 300 victories. If he had
surpassed 300, he'd be a shoo-in for the Hall of Fame. I hope
he makes it anyway.

Jim Perry pitched even better than the year before. In 1970
Perry won 24 games and was the first Twin to receive the
American League Cy Young Award. He came very close to
winning 25 games that year. In his final start of the season,
against Kansas City at Met Stadium, he blew a 5-0 lead in
the fifth inning. The Twins came back with two runs in the
last of the fifth and carried a 9-5 lead into the ninth, with
Perry still the pitcher of record. All Ron Perranoski, who
had another great year in relief for the Twins, had to do was
protect a four-run lead and Perry would have his 25th win.
But the Royals rallied with four singles. The Twins were still
up by two with two out, when Tovar, playing third, couldn't
handle a grounder hit by Lou Piniella. A run scored on the
error. Ed Kirkpatrick then doubled for two runs, putting the
Royals ahead. In that inning Tovar made another error, allowing another run. The Twins came back with two in the
last of the ninth and rallied with two in the last of the 11th,
tying the game again. It was a wild game, and the Twins set
a major-league record by using 27 players, but they lost in 12
innings. More significant than the loss, however, was the

missed chance for Perry at his 25th win.

There were a couple of odd events during the 1970 season. Bill Zepp, a Twins pitcher, wanted to be closer to his wife in Detroit. Since the Twins wouldn't trade him to the Tigers, he asked to be sent to the minors, since their top farm club was in Toledo, not far from Detroit. Zepp eventually got his first choice as he ended up with the Tigers in 1971. The other odd moment was at the Met in August 1970, when a game with Boston was suddenly stopped in the fourth inning. Public-address announcer Bob Casey explained that there was a bomb threat. We joined the players out in the middle of the field, as the officials figured we'd be safe out there if a bomb exploded in the stands. Most of the fans were ushered out to the parking lot, but some of them mingled with the players on the field. Vendors were walking through the infield and hawking popcorn and beer. No bomb exploded, and in less than an hour the game resumed.

The Twins faced Baltimore in the playoffs again in 1970, and although the Orioles were without a doubt the best team in baseball at this time, the Twins were optimistic because this time they would open the playoffs at home. But the Orioles swept the Twins decisively, outscoring them 27-10 in three games. Although the first two games, at the Met, ended with rather lopsided scores in favor of the Orioles, they were exciting. In each game the Orioles had a seven-run inning. In the second game, though, they didn't have their big inning until the ninth, and the Twins were trailing by just one run going into that inning.

In the first game the Orioles opened up a big lead with their seven runs in the fourth. They hit three home runs that inning, including a grand slam by pitcher Mike Cuellar. It was a strange one. Cuellar hit a high pop fly down the right-field line. It looked like a foul, but, aided by a strong wind, the ball just cleared the right-field fence at the foul pole. The first-base umpire, Bill Deegan, signaled a home run. Cuellar was so shocked that the plate umpire, John Stevens, gave him a little shove to start him running. Even though he helped himself to a big lead with that grand slam, Cuellar wasn't credited with the win for that game. The Twins rallied and knocked him out before he could complete the minimum five innings needed for a starter to receive a victory. I think that's the only game in which a starting pitcher hit a grand-slam home run but was so ineffective in pitching that he didn't get the win.

Everyone was disappointed at losing to the Orioles again, but were confident the Twins would have more chances in the playoffs in the future. As it turned out, it wouldn't be the near future.

Decline and Fall

Even though the Twins had won divisional titles in 1969 and 1970, in 1971 they finished 12 games under .500, in fifth place. In 1970 they were 61-29 against the teams in their own division, but in 1971 they dropped to 41-48. For the first time they drew fewer than one million fans. The season was not without its highlights, though, the most memorable being Harmon Killebrew's 500th home run. Harmon had hit 41 in 1970, his eighth season of topping 40, and he was just 13 shy of 500 coming into the 1971 season.

Harmon was expected to reach the milestone early in the season, but he struggled at the plate early in the year and then had some nagging injuries. To celebrate the event, the Twins scheduled July 6 as Mug Night, when they would give out a special mug commemorating Harmon's 500th home run. On July 6, however, Harmon was still a few home runs short, and he was on the disabled list. A month later, on August 9 in a game at the Met against Baltimore, Harmon hit his 500th homer, off Mike Cuellar. I was on the air at the time and announced that historic moment, and my partner, Ray Christensen, called number 501 later in the same game. Even after the slow start, Harmon finished the season with 28 home runs and led the league in RBIs with 119.

Unfortunately, it was still apparent at this time that Harmon was on the downside of his career. He never approached 40 home runs again and really had only one good year left in him, in 1972 when he hit 26 home runs. In 1973 he underwent midseason knee surgery and hit only five home runs. By 1974 he was being platooned, playing a little at first base but spending more time as a designated hitter. Harmon still thought he could play, but Cal Griffith thought otherwise. He offered Harmon some options, which included being a coach and part-time player with the Twins or managing one of the Twins' farm clubs. I think Calvin had it in mind that someday Killebrew might manage the Twins. But Harmon wanted to continue playing, so he asked for his release and signed with the Kansas City Royals for the 1975 season.

It was sad to see Harmon in another team's uniform, but he still gave us a couple of thrills at the Met in 1975. During the Royals' first trip to Minnesota the Twins arranged a ceremony to retire Harmon's number. Before one of the games, Halsey Hall presented Harmon with a framed uniform, showing his number 3, which no Twin would ever again wear. Then, his first time up in the game, Harmon homered into the left-field seats. It was just like old times, and even though he was now with an opposing team, he got a tremendous ovation from the fans as he circled the bases. Later in the season, in September, Harmon hit another homer at the Met. It was the last of his great career. When he retired at the end of the 1975 season, he had 573 home runs, fourth on the all-time list behind Hank Aaron, Babe Ruth, and Willie Mays, although Frank Robinson has since passed Harmon.

Besides Harmon's 500th home run in 1971, there were some other fine performances. Cesar Tovar had probably his best year ever, as he finished with a batting average of .311 and led the league with 204 hits. Tony Oliva, in the first half of the season, was hitting around .400 for a while. Then in a game at Oakland in late June he tried to make a sliding catch in right field, and seriously hurt his knee. Even though he missed much of the season, he led the American League in batting average and won his third batting title. Unfortunately, Tony was never the same after that season. He played only ten games in 1972, because he had so much trouble playing in the field. The American League adopted the designated hitter rule in 1973, so Tony was able to continue for a few more seasons, finishing his career as a DH, but he was only a shadow of his former self after the knee injury.

One other highlight of the 1971 season was the play of Leo Cardenas at shortstop. The trade for Cardenas after the 1968 season was one of Griffith's best. Cardenas had already done a steady job at shortstop for the Cincinnati Reds for many years. For Cardenas, the Twins traded left-hander Jim Merritt, who had a couple of good years in Cincinnati. He won 20 games for them in 1970 although he had an ERA of over four runs per game and definitely benefitted from the run support he got from his hitters, who became known as the "Big Red Machine." This trade helped both teams. The Reds got a good starting pitcher and the Twins a reliable shortstop, something they had lacked since the glory days of Zoilo Versalles.

In 1971 Leo set an American League record and tied the major-league record by making only 11 errors at shortstop, and he led the league in fielding percentage. Nevertheless, at the end of the season the Twins traded him to California for reliever Dave LaRoche. The Twins had guessed, correctly, that Cardenas had pretty much reached the end of the line, despite his outstanding season. In the final game of the 1971 season, at the Met, the Twins lost to California and missed a chance to finish at least in fourth place. During the game Cardenas got on base and was removed for a pinch runner. I think manager Bill Rigney did that so Cardenas could get a nice ovation from the fans. There weren't many people there, but they cheered as Cardenas ran off, perhaps sensing that he would not be back next year.

The Twins finished 26 games out of first place. Oakland led the division that year, helped by young Vida Blue, who won 24 games and received both the Cy Young and Most Valuable Player awards.

The Twins had a new look in 1972. They switched from their pinstripe to polyester uniforms, which followed the trend of other teams but weren't complimentary to large players like Killebrew. Instead of belts, the new uniforms had multicolored elastic waistbands making them look like pajamas. They weren't comfortable in hot weather, either. The Twins wore these uniforms for 15 years before switching back to a more traditional look in 1987, the year they won the World Series.

The 1972 season started late because of a player's strike, which delayed the start of the season by a couple of weeks. The Twins players worked out at St. Olaf College in Northfield during the strike.

Bobby Darwin joined the Twins in an off-season trade with the Dodgers. He was a big strong player and had been a pitcher for the Dodgers. His manager at Triple-A ball in the Pacific Coast League had been Tommy Lasorda, a former pitcher himself. Lasorda figured that Darwin would not make it to the big leagues as a pitcher, but he had watched Darwin taking batting practice and was impressed with his power with the bat. So Lasorda called the Dodgers' front office in Los Angeles and asked for permission to try Darwin in the outfield. The front office agreed, and it turned out to be a very good move.

Darwin got off to a fast start with the Twins, hitting six home runs in early May. Then the pitchers discovered his

I was thrilled to get the job of broadcasting Twins games on WCCO.
WCCO Radio.

Even after he became vice president, Hubert Humphrey
would join us in the broadcast booth every so often.
He was quite a fan. *WCCO Radio.*

Mr. Indestructible: Bob Allison. *WCCO Radio.*

Rod Carew was the American League's Rookie of the Year in 1967.
He won a total of seven American League batting titles.
We're still good friends. *Jerry Stebbins*

Dean Chance came to the Twins in 1967 and pitched a couple
of no-hitters (although one was shortened by rain). *WCCO Radio.*

Rich Reese hit a memorable grand slam off Dave McNally
of the Orioles in 1969. *WCCO Radio.*

weakness: curveballs. Still, he had a few pretty good years with the Twins and, when he did connect, he could send the ball a long way. In 1974, he launched a homer into the second deck of the left-field seats at the Met, the only player besides Killebrew ever to do that.

Darwin wasn't a bad fielder but he had one afternoon in 1972 he'd just as soon forget. Dick Allen was in his first season with the White Sox. He won the American League Most Valuable Player award and set a team record with 37 home runs. Two of those homers were hit on a Monday afternoon at the Met in late July 1972. His first time up Allen hit a sinking, knuckleballing line drive to center. Darwin ran in and tried to make a sliding shoestring catch. He missed, and the ball skipped by him and rolled all the way to the center-field fence, as Allen circled the bases with an inside-the-park home run. Later in the game Allen hit an almost identical shot, for another inside-the-park home run. No one had hit two inside-the-park home runs in a single game in nearly 40 years. Ironically, it wouldn't be the last time I would see something like that happen. Near the end of the 1986 season Greg Gagne of the Twins had a pair of inside jobs at the Metrodome.

Jim Kaat was going great for the Twins in 1972. He was 10-2 with an ERA of just over two, when he broke a bone in his pitching hand after sliding into second base. Despite their good start in 1972, the Twins slumped in May and June. In July, Griffith fired Rigney as manager and gave the job to Frank Quilici, who had been a very popular player and then coach with the Twins. Quilici had no managing experience, not even at the minor-league level, but Griffith decided to take a chance on him. Harmon Killebrew gave Frank a nice present in his first game as manager. The Yankees were up by a run in the seventh inning, when Harmon hit a two-run homer to put the Twins ahead and help them win in Quilici's debut.

The next day Mel Stottlemyre of the Yankees and Bert Blyleven each pitched ten scoreless innings before the Yankees won the game on a home run by Bernie Allen, a former Twin. It was a long day because the game went extra innings and because the start of the game had been delayed by rain for more than two hours. As Knothole Day fans were waiting out the delay in the left-field seats, Mike Kekich, a Yankee pitcher, ran some wind sprints in the rain. At first the fans hooted at Kekich, who began doing slides and belly flops on the wet turf. The fans cheered him, and Kekich quit running and led the cheers. The fans loved it, and I'll always remember Mike Kekich, who went out of his way to provide some fun and entertainment for the fans. (Kekich is remembered by most others for something else; after the 1972 season, he and fellow Yankee pitcher Fritz Peterson swapped wives.)

The Twins finished the 1972 season at .500 with a record of 77-77, having played only 154 games instead of the usual 162 because of the strike at the beginning of the year. The Twins then got into the trade mart in a big way. They dealt away several veterans, including Jim Perry and Cesar Tovar. For two pitchers from the Cubs they traded Dave LaRoche, whom they had just acquired a year before in the Cardenas deal. They traded Rick Dempsey, a young catcher, for Danny Walton from the Yankees. Walton had hit 17 home runs with the Brewers in 1970, but afterward he never hit more than four homers in a season. Meanwhile, Rick Dempsey had a good career as a catcher with several teams. In an outstanding deal the Twins traded right-handed reliever Wayne Granger to the Cardinals for lefty John Cumberland, who didn't have a very long career in the big leagues, and outfielder Larry Hisle, who played some great ball with the Twins.

In another change after the 1972 season, we learned that Halsey Hall would not be back in the broadcast crew in 1973. Halsey was 74, and apparently the station and the team felt that all the travel might be too much for him. I don't think Halsey was entirely happy with the decision.

Halsey

I met Halsey Hall in 1961, when I was in my last year of broadcasting for Baltimore. When the Orioles played their last season of the series in Minnesota, it was already known that Bob Wolff would be leaving the Twins broadcast crew and there would be an opening for another announcer. Halsey told me that I was under consideration to replace Wolff and that he and Scotty (his name for Ray Scott) were rooting for me. I got the Twins job and got to know Halsey.

I soon sensed Halsey's popularity. He had already had a long career in sports broadcasting and writing in the Twin Cities by the time he joined the Twins broadcast crew at the age of 62. There's a debate as to what announcer was the first to use the phrase "Holy Cow!" It has been attributed to Harry Caray, now with the Chicago Cubs, and Phil Rizzuto of the Yankees, but I'm told Halsey was using the expression long before either of them became broadcasters.

With his great recall of baseball stories, Halsey was a terrific partner, especially during a rain delay. Nowadays when a game is interrupted, we turn the airwaves over to the studio, but when I started with the Twins, we'd have to fill the time ourselves. As long as Halsey was there that was never a problem. Many fans from those days say that often their favorite part of a game was a rain delay filled with Halsey's stories. He often talked about the Minneapolis Millers and the St. Paul Saints, the minor-league teams that preceded the Twins game. And he was also in demand from the opposing team's broadcast crew, who knew that no one could fill rain delays better than Halsey, so he developed a following in other American League cities as well.

Even though the fans loved the chance to be regaled by Halsey when a game was interrupted by rain, Halsey himself didn't like to see a game delayed. He'd say, "What are the umpires wearing tonight? Paper suits?" The only time I remember when he agreed with an umpire's decision to stop a game was on a night at Met Stadium when a tornado touched down half a mile from the park. Halsey also disliked day games because they interfered with midday soap operas. After a day game Halsey always asked people what he'd missed on his favorite soaps.

Besides "Holy Cow!" Halsey's trademarks included green onions, cigars, distilled beverages, and a fear of flying. He chomped on green onions in the broadcast booth and claimed they were great for his health. Maybe they were, but they didn't do much for the rest of us. And he was constantly smoking cigars. I often said that Halsey always enjoyed a good cigar; unfortunately, those weren't the kind he smoked.

He was known for starting fires with his cigar. The most famous incident occurred in 1968 during a doubleheader against the White Sox in Chicago. A large pile of Western Union ticker tape had built up on the floor over the course of the afternoon, and one of the ashes from Halsey's cigar ignited the pile. Merle Harmon was on the air with him, so I was in another part of the press box, but I saw quite a commotion in the radio booth. By the time they extinguished the ticker-tape fire, Halsey's sport coat, draped over his chair, had burned, too. When the Twins catcher Jerry Zimmerman heard the story, he quipped, "Halsey's the only man I know who can turn a sport coat into a blazer."

Halsey was also fond of a good drink, and on road trips he lugged along a satchel full of liquor bottles. Whenever anyone ever asked him about the contents of his bag, Halsey said it contained reference books. Dave Mona, who covered the Twins for the Minneapolis Tribune in the late 1960s, commented, "those were the first reference books I ever knew of that clinked."

Once a young reporter asked him why he bothered carrying his own liquor since every town they visited had a bar.

"My boy," Halsey replied, "you never know when you'll run into a local election."

Halsey was especially prone to take a nip whenever he boarded an airplane. He was quite nervous about flying, and he referred to his liquor as "flight medicine." He used to make road trips by train, but when he became a Twins announcer, with few off days and long distances between some of the American League cities, he had to fly regularly. When buying a plane ticket, he might ask for "one chance to Cleveland." One time in the airport when Halsey was waiting for his flight, some of his colleagues, as a joke, arranged for the pilot to walk past with a seeing-eye dog.

During spring training one year Halsey learned too late that he could have avoided a bumpy flight from Charlotte, North Carolina, to Knoxville, Tennessee. The Twins had just completed training camp at their base in Orlando, Florida, and were about to play some more exhibition games before the regular season opened. We had just flown through some rough weather from Orlando to Charlotte, only to find that the game in Charlotte had been canceled because of the bad weather. Since there would be no game in Charlotte, the flight to Knoxville for the next game would leave in a couple of hours. Sid Hartman, a columnist for one of the Minneapolis newspapers, decided to avoid another bumpy flight, especially since this flight over the Smoky Mountains might be even rougher. So Sid and another writer, Max Nichols, rented a car and invited me along. I accepted and offered to drive. I knew the area pretty well, having often driven through the Smoky or Blue Ridge Mountains, and I knew that Halsey would be delighted to join us and avoid the flight. But we couldn't find him, not at the Charlotte ballpark, the railroad station, or anywhere. We had a very pleasant trip over the Smoky Mountains. When we arrived in Knoxville, though, Halsey was waiting in the hotel lobby. He had heard about our car and was annoyed that we hadn't invited him along. We explained how hard we had scoured Charlotte, but I don't think we ever convinced him.

Halsey had a reputation for frugality, which I think he cultivated as a sort of Jack Benny persona. Whenever a group of us went out to eat, he always insisted upon separate checks. I first observed Halsey's frugality in 1962 during a road trip with him in New York. At the Roosevelt Hotel the elevator operator often had a stack of newspapers for sale. One night after a game at Yankee Stadium, as we rode up the elevator, Halsey took a copy of the early edition of the next day's paper and put a dime on the stack. "Excuse me, sir," the elevator operator said. "On the elevator the newspapers are 15 cents."

Halsey thought about it for a few seconds, picked up his dime, put back the paper, and said, "I'll be blamed if I'll pay 15 cents for a ten-cent newspaper." He waited until the next morning and bought the paper for a dime at the newsstand.

Some years later, when Ray Christensen broadcast Twins games with us, we were in County Stadium in Milwaukee. During the course of the broadcast Ray mentioned a conversation he had with one of the players on the team bus coming over to the ballpark. Between innings Halsey grabbed Ray by the arm, shook him a little, and said, "For Pete's sake, don't be saying anything on the air about us taking the team bus. The station thinks I take a cab."

In Baltimore one night Halsey, Ray Scott, and I ate dinner at the Eager House. Howard Fox, the Twins' traveling secretary, was in a nearby booth with some of his friends. When the check was delivered, Halsey was taken aback. He called the waiter over, asked him to add up the figures again, and asked, "What are you trying to do—put the chef on a pension?"

The waiter pulled out his pencil, checked the addition, and said, "No sir, this is the correct amount."

Halsey reached for his wallet and discovered it wasn't in his pocket. At the time, we didn't know he had left it at the hotel, so he stood up and tapped his water glass with his spoon. "Ladies and gentlemen," he announced, "I want you to know that this is the biggest clip joint I've ever been in. Not only do they pad the check, but they also pick your pocket!"

Halsey was generous and thoughtful, though. A couple of weeks after Kathy and I moved to Minnesota, Halsey and his wife, Sula, gave us a delightful house-warming gift: a deluxe antique stereoscope with a cylinder for turning the pictures.

Halsey always had a funny line for any occasion. Once I asked him if he liked all sports when he was growing up.

"Yes, I did. Baseball was my favorite, far and away my favorite, but as for participating in anything, I suppose track was my best sport."

I said, "Oh really, I didn't know about that."

"Yes, and I don't want to sound immodest, but I still hold my high school's team record for the high jump."

"Gee, that's great," I said. "Still the record after all these years?"

"Oh yeah, I'll never forget it. It was the day I backed into the javelin."

Although Halsey was masterful with words, on occasion, he was the master of malaprops. Once, telling listeners about that game's promotional gift, a pair of pantyhose for every woman there, he said, "In promotions here tonight, fans, it was *pantywaist* night." He was puzzled when I broke into laughter and asked, "What are you laughing about? You didn't get any, did you?"

Halsey had a way of reaching over and taking your stat sheet or other notes during a game so he could read them. He'd often forget to give them back, and later you'd find your notes on the floor or even in the wastebasket.

Sometimes Halsey had trouble adjusting to technological advances in broadcasting such as the cough switch, for deactivating a microphone. Halsey never used it. To prevent certain comments from going over the air, he would cover his microphone—with just one finger. Fortunately, he never said anything very objectionable.

Once he did the reverse: he was announcing a game, but his words weren't making the airwaves. For a spring-training game in West Palm Beach, Florida, the radio engineer assumed there would be just one announcer, so he had brought only one microphone. When he discovered he needed another, he gave us a lavaliere microphone, designed to be clipped on the shirt. Halsey didn't feel like clipping it on since he moved around so much in the booth, so he laid it on the counter to pick up when he needed it. Suddenly the engineer was punching me and pointing at Halsey. Instead of the microphone, Halsey was talking into a stopwatch. When he discovered his mistake, Halsey burst into fits of laughter, and I announced, "Halsey has just revolutionized radio."

A little later the engineer whispered to me, "Is this old guy just starting in radio?"

"As a matter of fact," I said, "he started about 40 years ago."

This engineer wasn't the only person Halsey left a bit bewildered. Once after a game in Boston I was leaving Fenway Park and saw Halsey standing on a corner outside the stadium. I asked if he was going back to the hotel, The Somerset, about six blocks away, and said I'd walk back with him. Halsey said he was tired and thought he'd grab a cab instead.

Okay," I said, "but you're not going to get a cab on this corner. They don't come this way. You'll have to go down to the next corner."

As we walked to the corner, I saw a cab turn and head our way. There was a truck parked on our side of the street, and I had to duck around the truck to hail the cab. When the cab stopped, I got in and left the back door open for Halsey. He came around from behind the truck, looked in the back seat of the cab, and said to the driver, "Oh, pardon me. I didn't know you had a passenger."

As he walked away, I jumped out of the cab and yelled, "Halsey, come on, will you? Here's the cab."

"We can't take that cab," Halsey said. "He's already got a passenger."

One time in the early 1960s Halsey rented a car in Los Angeles. The stadium there was called Dodger Stadium only for Dodger games; for Angel games it was known as Chavez Ravine. (The crowds at Chavez Ravine were never as large as the crowds at Dodger Stadium.) After an Angels night game there Halsey offered me a ride back to the hotel. We straightened up the radio booth and were among the last people to leave. In the Chavez Ravine parking lot we drove to an the exit gate, but there was a barricade in front of it. We then tried two other exits but found them barricaded, too. We wondered if the keepers of the stadium had assumed everyone was gone and had closed all the gates. As he continued driving around, Halsey was muttering that he'd send the Angels' management a bill for the mileage he was putting on the car. Finally, I spotted another car moving through the lot. "Halsey, follow that car," I said. "Maybe he knows where to get out." And sure enough, that car drove through the one gate still open, and we were close on his tail.

Halsey rented another car once, and at night on the freeway we ran very low on fuel.

Halsey, peering down the road, asked, "Is that a Shell station ahead?"

"No, Halsey," I replied, "that's a full moon."

A few years after he retired from full-time announcing in 1972, there was a dinner to roast Halsey. I was unable to attend, but I sent a letter to be read by the master of ceremonies, Howard Viken of WCCO Radio:

> First, Halsey, just a brief explanation as to my absence. You see, I had to choose between either being at your party or accepting an invitation to be a judge in the All-World Halitosis Contest. The sponsors of the Halitosis Contest felt that, having worked with you for eleven years with your cigars, garlic, and onions, I was extremely well qualified to be a judge.
>
> When I first joined you and Ray Scott as a member of the Twins' broadcasting team in 1962, I was amazed at what good health you were in. The only defect you seemed to have was an apparent kidney problem. You never said anything about this, but I noticed that whenever we went out to eat and you saw the waiter coming with the check, you'd have to go to the men's room.
>
> Since you haven't been on the Twins broadcasts, attendance at the games has declined considerably. The reason is

obvious: when you were announcing the games, people had to come out to the ballpark to find out what was really going on.

Halsey, you were in the broadcast business for over 50 years, and in the time I've known you you've always been one of the most humble men I've ever met. But let's face it, Halsey, you've got a lot to be humble about.

> Your long-suffering sidekick,
> Herb Carneal

I'm told that the audience laughed as Howard Viken read the letter. But, as was to be expected, nobody laughed harder than Halsey.

Even though 1972 was Halsey's last year as a regular member of the broadcast crew, he wasn't gone completely. Hal Greenwood of Midwest Federal, at that time the main sponsor for the Twins' broadcasts, hired Halsey to be an Ambassador of Baseball. At Met Stadium Halsey presided over pregame ceremonies on special occasions such as Opening Day, and he joined us on some of the home broadcasts. Even when he didn't have a specific assignment, Halsey was usually in the press box during games. He served as Ambassador of Baseball until his death in 1977.

In 1979 when the *Minneapolis Star* surveyed its readers to determine the most popular local celebrities, Halsey was voted the top sportscaster of the 1970s, even though the poll was taken two years after his death.

Tony Oliva won batting titles in his first two full seasons
in the majors. *WCCO Radio.*

Change-ups

With Halsey, our color analyst, gone in 1973, Ray Christensen and I alternated between play-by-play and color work. In the past, whichever play-by-play man wasn't on the air could take a break. Now, we'd have to remain on the air all the time, doing one or the other.

The 1973 season also was the year they started the designated hitter in the American League. No longer would pitchers have to hit, and instead they could be replaced by a batter who would not have to play the field. The Yankees' Ron Blomberg was the first man to bat as a designated hitter, because the game, in the Eastern time zone, started earlier than most other games in the league. Tony Oliva of the Twins was the first designated hitter to hit a home run. The DH rule added years to Tony's career, and he knocked in 92 runs that year.

At first I disapproved of such a radical change in a game known for not making radical changes, but as time went on, I appreciated its good features, since the DH rule allowed guys like Tony Oliva to keep going. Nevertheless, purists, like me, are still bothered by the DH rule. One objection is that the DH reduces strategy, because a manager no longer has to decide whether to use a pinch hitter for a pitcher who is still pitching well but trailing in the seventh inning. But how often does this come up, especially when it might be a difficult decision? These days, starting pitchers don't often pitch beyond seven innings anyway. Now the decision on whether to relieve a pitcher is based on how he's pitching and how tired he is.

Bert Blyleven had an excellent year in 1973, winning 20 games for the only time in his career. He was 20-17, and a lot of those losses resulted from a shortage of Twins runs. Bert's earned-run average in 1973 was 2.52, so clearly with some decent run support from his hitters he could have won many more than 20 games.

This was the year of the phenom breaking in. When the Twins were in Texas in June, 18-year-old pitcher David Clyde, a high-school sensation, made his debut just after being signed by the Rangers. That drew a big crowd, and the Twins decided to do the same thing. Their top pick in the free-agent draft had been Eddie Bane, a southpaw from Arizona State who had beaten the Minnesota Gophers in the College World Series in early June. After the Twins signed Bane, they decided to give him a shot with the big leagues right away and announced he would start the Fourth of July game against Kansas City. The Met was sold out for his debut. Bane was a lot of fun to watch. In his windup he turned all the way around, so he was facing center field, before coiling back to deliver the pitch, much like a left-handed Luis Tiant. He did well in his first game, pitching seven strong innings, although the Twins lost. Unfortunately, like David Clyde, he had a very disappointing career in the majors.

Jim Kaat struggled in 1973, trying to come back from his hand injury. Near the end of the season he was released, leaving only Killebrew as a member of the original Twins, and signed with the Chicago White Sox. Jim won 21 games for the Sox in 1974, and in 1975 he had another 20-win season. In Chicago, he was reunited with his favorite pitching coach, Johnny Sain, who helped him develop a very effective quick-delivery style: as soon as Jim received the ball back from his catcher, he would fire again, allowing the batter little time to get set up in the box. Batters did what they could to slow Kaat down, by stepping out of the box and calling time. But Jim continued working quickly, and whenever Kaat pitched, you could count on an extremely fast game.

Griffith took a lot of heat for giving up too soon on Kaat after Kitty had those good seasons in Chicago, and the fans and writers also pointed out that Griffith had released Luis Tiant after the 1970 season. Tiant had been acquired from Cleveland after the 1969 season, and he won his first six games with the Twins in 1970 before he was injured. After being released from the Twins, Tiant went on to have some great seasons, mainly with the Red Sox. But critics should remember that many other teams passed on Tiant after his injury. Although Calvin released a few good players, his overall record in trades has been very good.

Near the end of the 1973 season Nolan Ryan of the California Angels set a major-league record by striking out 383 batters that year, breaking Sandy Koufax's previous record of 382. Going into a game against the Twins on September 27 in Anaheim, Ryan needed 16 strikeouts to break the record. Nobody thought he would get that many in this game, but he was scheduled to pitch again, with two days rest, in the final game of the season on September 30.

Ryan was hot this night. In the eighth inning he got his 15th strikeout of the game, tying Koufax's mark. He also pulled something in his leg that inning and was having difficulty pushing off the mound. Without his fastball he didn't strike anyone out in the ninth or tenth innings. Then with two out in the 11th, he fired three strikes past Rich Reese. The Angels won the game in the last of the 11th, so Ryan's final pitch to Reese was his final pitch of the season.

The Twins finished at .500 again in 1973. Ray Christensen's contract was not renewed after that season. Ray was deemed "too frank" in some of his comments about the Twins' play over the last two seasons. Ray has never been afraid to tell it like it is, but he's been able to handle the last 25 years of mediocre football at the University of Minnesota without being accused of being too frank. And in 1973 you couldn't have found many people who would say the Twins were playing well.

My new partner, Larry Calton, had sent quite a detailed job application, in which he claimed that he injected so much excitement into his announcing that the fans would be fired up and attendance at the Met would be at least a million. The Twins had last drawn a million in 1970, but Calton said that if the Twins did not draw a million in 1974, he would give back half his salary.

Well, the fans weren't any more enthusiastic than they had been during the last few years, and going into the last home game of the year, their season attendance stood at 660,000. In the press box just before that final game Pat Reusse, a writer for the St. Paul Pioneer Press, said to me in a loud voice as Calton walked by, "Well, Herb, it looks like your partner might be in a little financial difficulty if the Twins don't draw 340,000 fans today." The crowd that day was barely over 2,000, and the Twins ended the year with their worst attendance since coming to Minnesota. I don't know whether Larry gave back half his salary.

Calton's high-decibel style did not go over with the fans, and he embellished the plays too much. He'd turn a routine fly ball into a long drive caught on the warning track. A lot of fans bring radios to the ballpark with them. They'd hear Larry distort a play that they could see for themselves; when that happens, an announcer quickly loses credibility. Calvin Griffith gave me some good advice early on: "Keep one thing in mind," he said. "Your job is to tell the people what's going on down on the field."

Larry played a little minor-league ball and then had done some announcing at the Triple-A level in Tulsa and Oklahoma City and had filled in on a few St. Louis Cardinals games. Some years later, in announcing a University of Evansville basketball game, he berated an official and got a technical foul called on him—a rather rare penalty for a radio announcer. One time when Vic Albury was pitching and getting hit pretty hard, Larry said on the air, "How long are they going to leave Albury in there? If he threw his fastball into a windowpane, the ball would bounce back to him." Albury later heard about Larry's comments and was ready to punch Larry's lights out.

One player, Danny Walton, did punch him out. In the middle of the 1975 season we were on the team bus taking us from the hotel to the stadium in Texas. I always sit up front, while the players gravitate to the rear. If I want to talk to a player, I go back there, but Calton sat with the players. Danny Walton was passing out cigars, because his wife had just had a baby after a difficult pregnancy. Larry took a cigar, congratulated Danny, and added a wisecrack about who the real father was. At the ballpark I was one of the first in the clubhouse. A few seconds later I heard a loud noise and turned. Larry was on the floor. Walton had belted him. Larry jumped up and grabbed something, a mop or a broom, as if to hit Walton. Frank Quilici grabbed Calton and told him he was banned from the clubhouse for the rest of the season. That move was extremely popular with the players.

From the time Frank Quilici took over managing the team in the middle of 1972 through 1974, the Twins had been winning as many as they lost. Their hopes for 1975 rested on their pitching staff led by Bert Blyleven. Rookie pitcher Jim Hughes, known as Blue Gill, had been called up by the

Twins near the end of the 1974 season and finished his year in grand fashion.

In the first inning of this game the Rangers' Toby Harrah hit a grounder that went right through Eric Soderholm at third. It looked like an error, but official scorer Bob Fowler, a columnist with the *Minneapolis Star*, called it a hit. As the innings wore on, Jim Hughes was setting down the Rangers without another hit. Meanwhile, the Twins' dugout was giving Fowler a lot of heat to change his call.

Buck Rodgers, a coach with the Twins, called Fowler and asked, "Can you change the hit to an error?"

"I can," Fowler said, "but I won't."

Billy Martin, who was managing Texas, called Fowler and said the Rangers would have no problem if he changed his call. Fowler stuck to his guns.

Then with two out in the ninth Pete Mackanin of the Rangers tripled for their second hit of the game. Even though he didn't have a no-hitter, Hughes finished with a shutout, and Fowler could not be blamed for denying him a no-hitter. A few years later when the Twins acquired Mackanin, Fowler wrote a column on how much he owed Mackanin for getting him off the hook.

In 1975 Hughes had a scoreless streak in May. In the game when Killebrew homered for the Royals in the first inning after his number was retired before the game, Hughes came into the game in relief in the third and pitched seven scoreless innings for the win.

A week and a half later Hughes pitched a four-hit shutout against Cleveland. In that game Rod Carew stole home in the first inning. Gaylord Perry, on the mound for the Indians, seemed to have been challenging him to try it. With Carew on third Perry had continued to work out of a windup. On each pitch Carew took a few steps down the line. Finally, he did get a good jump as Perry went into his

148

windup and slid in ahead of the catcher's tag. On Rod's next time up, Perry's first pitch was way inside, obviously intended as a message that he didn't like it that Carew had stolen home. Rod wasn't happy about it, so on the next pitch Rod swung and missed, and his bat flew out of his hands toward Perry. When Rod retrieved his bat, he pointed it right at Perry and let him know he didn't appreciate what he had just done. First-base umpire Nestor Chylak asked him if the bat had slipped from his hands. Rod said, "Did you ask Gaylord if that pitch slipped?"

In his next start, Hughes shut out the Milwaukee Brewers at the Met and became the second Twin to pitch back-to-back shutouts. Camilo Pascual was the first, and since then Frank Viola and Scott Erickson have done it. Hughes was almost victimized by Robertson's Roost, a new innovation at the Met. Before the season started, the Twins put up an eight-foot-high fence in left field 15 feet in front of the permanent stands, shortening the distance down the line from 346 to 331 feet. This shorter porch was the idea of Twins' vice president Billy Robertson, who hoped it might help the Twins to hit more home runs. But with few long-ball hitters the Twins weren't likely to benefit as much as the big hitters on the visiting teams. In the ninth inning of Hughes' game against Milwaukee, light-hitting Tim Johnson lifted a long fly to left, but Twins' left-fielder Steve Braun ran back, stationed himself in front of the new fence, and jumped high to snag the ball, robbing Johnson of a home run and preserving Blue Gill's shutout. This was as close as Tim Johnson ever came to hitting a home run in his six-year career in the majors. Jim Hughes finished the season with 16 wins. Another young pitcher, Dave Goltz, a Minnesota native, finished at 14-14, his third straight year with a .500 record. After one more .500 season he broke though with a 20-win season in 1977. Goltz pitched longer, eight years, than any other Twin without ever having a losing season. That's sometimes a little trivia question I like to throw at people.

Blyleven had another good season, finishing at 15-10. The Twins played well through the end of May, but then the pitching suffered a letdown, and only Carew was hitting well. He had another great year, winning his third-straight batting title and his fourth overall, hitting .359, just a few points shy of his .364 average the year before. Even with Robertson's Roost the Twins finished eighth in the league in home runs. One of those homers was by Tom Kelly, who would later manage the Twins. During his only season in the majors Kelly, a first baseman, played in 49 games with 23 hits in 127 at-bats, including that home run, which came off Detroit's Vern Ruhle at Tiger Stadium.

After a bad midseason slump, the Twins rallied and played some good ball near the end of the 1975 season, but they finished seven games under .500. As soon as the season ended, Cal Griffith announced that Quilici would not be back. During his seasons as manager, the Twins were hampered by many injuries. Sometimes the team was short-handed, even in September, when teams could expand their rosters to 40 players. Calvin Griffith often seemed reluctant to call up players from the minor leagues. At the end of the season Frank had just 22 players in uniform, and one of them, Steve Brye, with his wrist in a cast, could do nothing but pinch run.

After that season Danny Thompson wrote a book, an exposé along the lines of *Ball Four*, Jim Bouton's controversial best-seller about his year with the Seattle Pilots and Houston Astros in 1969. Thompson's book wasn't as juicy as Bouton's and sold far fewer copies, but it still raised a few eyebrows. As an announcer, I have always tried to honor the privilege of being allowed into the clubhouse, and I certainly would never try to write a book about what went on in there.

In 1976 my broadcast partner Larry Calton was replaced by Frank Quilici. Calvin Griffith thought Frank would do well on the air because he knew baseball and related to people very well. Since Frank had never done play-by-play, for the first six weeks of the season, Frank did the color work while I called the action. In the middle of May at a double-header in Anaheim, I did the play-by-play for the first game and half the second. By this time I was bushed, and since it was about one o'clock in the morning back in the Twin Cities, there were probably few listeners, so it seemed a good time for Frank to get his feet wet. I gave him no warning, so he wouldn't have time to become nervous. When we came out of a commercial, I said, "And now for the play-by-play, here's Frank Quilici." He was a little shocked, but he went right ahead announcing. We always helped each other out. He knew more about baseball, and I was more experienced as an announcer. We were partners through 1982, although he took a couple years off, 1978 and 1979.

The Twins' new manager in 1976 was Gene Mauch, well known in the area because he had played for the minor-league St. Paul Saints and later had been a player-manager for the Minneapolis Millers. He had successfully managed the Philadelphia Phillies and then the Montreal Expos. His reputation as a disciplinarian appealed to Griffith, and in November 1975, Mauch signed a three-year contract to manage the team, the longest contract ever granted to a Twins' manager up to that time.

Among other changes, Carew moved from second to first base. Carew had been severely injured turning a double play in 1970, and the Twins were afraid of another such mishap. They finally eliminated that risk by moving him to first. Immediately at home in his new position, he had as successful a career there as he'd had at second. The Twins also brought up Butch Wynegar, a 19-year-old switch-hitting catcher whose only previous professional experience had been with Reno, Nevada, in the Class A California League, where Butch had hit 19 home runs with 112 RBIs. Butch had a great start with the Twins, and that year he became the youngest player ever in the All-Star Game.

In 1976 the Twins ended up leading the league in runs scored, even though they hit only 81 home runs. The weak output was indicative of the entire American League. The Red Sox, playing in cozy Fenway Park, led the league with just 134 home runs, and Graig Nettles of the Yankees was the individual league leader with 32 home runs. The Twins' leader in homers was Danny Ford with 20.

Another development was that baseball's reserve clause had been overturned by an arbitrator in late 1975. The reserve clause had bound a player to a particular team for as long as that team wanted him. The new era of free agency resulted in the loss of several Twins players in the following years. The first to play out his option and go was reliever Bill Campbell, who had a 17-5 record with 20 saves for the Twins in 1976 but at the end of the season was free to look elsewhere. He ended up signing with the Boston Red Sox.

Even before Campbell's departure, the new system influenced the Twins to trade off Bert Blyleven, their best pitcher. Early in the season Griffith had concluded that at the end of the year he would lose Blyleven to free agency and get nothing in return, so in June he traded him to the Texas Rangers, along with Danny Thompson, for pitchers Bill Singer and Jim Gideon, third baseman Mike Cubbage, and shortstop Roy Smalley, who happened to be Gene Mauch's nephew. Mauch said to me, "I can't believe how much we got in return." Although Gideon, a minor-leaguer at the time, never pitched for the Twins, the other three players, especially

Smalley, made excellent contributions to the team. Blyleven was booed as he was taken out of a game in his final Twins appearance. In response Bert made an obscene gesture. For many years he was booed whenever he pitched against the Twins at the Met.

Mike Cubbage played a few seasons at third and attracted one of the most vocal fan clubs ever at the Met. A few seasons earlier catcher Phil Roof's fan club sat out in the right-field bleachers by the bullpen, near Roof, who rarely played. The Mike Cubbage Fan Club hung out in "Cubby's Corner," in the second-deck box seats near third base, where Cubbage played. In those days fans could sit almost anywhere they wanted because of the low attendance at the Met. This wild bunch sang their "We Love You, Cubby" song with great gusto. Sometimes they sang near our broadcast booth so it went out over the air, and Frank Quilici joined in the song. Otherwise, Met Stadium was a pretty quiet place back then.

The Twins got off to a slow start in 1976, and although they finished only five games out of first, they were never in the pennant race. But there had been quite a race for the batting title. Rod Carew was looking for his fourth-straight crown even though a slump early in the season had hurt his chances. Going into the final game of the year, he still had a chance, along with Lyman Bostock, in his second season with the Twins. Their two main competitors were also teammates, George Brett and Hal McRae of the Kansas City Royals.

The Twins' final game was at Kansas City, with these four players still vying for the lead in batting average. As the game wore on, Carew and Bostock dropped out of contention, but Brett and McRae were neck-and-neck going into the last of the ninth. If Brett got a hit and McRae came up empty, Brett would win the title. Brett, a left-handed hitter, looped a fly ball into left-center field. Steve Brye, playing left field for the Twins, ran in but then pulled up. The ball landed in front of him and bounced over his head, and Brett circled the bases with an inside-the-park home run. McRae came up next and made an out, so Brett won the batting title.

McRae was enraged and made a gesture toward Mauch. McRae, who is black, charged that the Twins had helped Brett because he is white. Mauch, infuriated at the accusation, came out of the dugout, and he and McRae had to be restrained.

The Mike Cubbage Fan Club had some fun with that incident the next year, when left fielder Steve Brye was no longer with the Twins. When the Royals came to the Met for the first time in 1977, the Cubby's Corner bunch put up two signs. One, on the facing of the second-deck infield stands read, "Bring Back Steve Brye," and had a drawing of an outfielder dropping a fly and saying "Oops!" The other sign read, "Hal McRae Fan Club: Members Only," and they put it in the deepest reaches of the second-deck outfield stands, where no one was sitting.

There was one other game that almost proved to be memorable in 1976. It came in August when Steve Luebber almost pitched the Twins' first no-hitter since 1967.

Luebber had joined the Twins in 1971 but had spent most of his time in the minors since then. Now in 1976, on a Saturday night in Texas, he held the Rangers hitless into the ninth. He quickly retired Gene Clines and Lenny Randle, who was pinch-hitting for Danny Thompson. Then he got Roy Howell to swing and miss at his first two pitches. It looked pretty good for Luebber at this point, with two out and an 0-2 count on the batter. Howell stayed alive by fouling off a pitch, then worked the count to 2-and-2. The fans by this time were chanting, "Break it! Break it!" and Howell did just that, lining a pitch over Luebber's head into center field to spoil the no-hit bid. Mike Hargrove followed with another hit, and Luebber was taken out of the game. He still got the win, but you can imagine how difficult that must be, how tough it is to come that close to a no-hitter and then not get it. But that was the case with Steve Luebber, who didn't have a very notable major-league career. But he did come close to that one moment of glory in Texas.

Roy Smalley makes the final out of the last game at Met Stadium.
Fans roamed the field after the game, not wanting to leave.
WCCO Radio.

The Final Years at the Met

The 1977 season was exciting for the Twins, even though they ended in fourth place. This was the year of the "Lumber Company" with heavy hitters like Lyman Bostock, Danny Ford, Glenn Adams, Craig Kusick, Larry Hisle, who led the league with 119 RBIs, and, of course, Rod Carew. The Twins led the league in runs scored, setting a team record of 867 runs, averaging nearly five and a half per game. They led the Western Division for 51 days and stayed in contention until mid-September. For most of the year they were battling with Chicago for the top spot, although both teams faded near the end, and Kansas City won the division for the second-straight year. Chicago came in third, followed by the Twins, with a record of 84-77. Even though they finished 17 games behind the Royals, the Twins had generated enough excitement to draw more than a million fans to the Met for the first time since 1970.

Perhaps the high point of the season was the game with the White Sox at the Met on the last Sunday in June. The Sox had won the previous day, moving ahead of the Twins into first place. A sellout crowd turned out for the final game of the series the next day, when the promotional gift was a replica Rod Carew jersey for the young fans.

The Twins opened up a big lead with a six-run second inning, including a grand slam by Glenn Adams, who finished the game with eight RBIs, setting a team record which has since been tied by Randy Bush. The White Sox came back with six runs of their own in the third. The Twins won, 19-12, and took over first place again. There was a little of everything in the game, including a fan being ejected after he climbed all the way to the top of the foul pole in left field while the game was in progress in the fourth inning. The White Sox announcers at the time were Harry Caray and Jimmy Piersall. Piersall had had some mental problems during his playing days, and even after he'd overcome them, he was known as something of a flake. As the authorities were trying to get the fan down off the foul pole, sportswriter Pat Reusse banged on the Chicago broadcast booth and hollered, "Hey, Harry, tell Piersall to get down from there!" (Of course, it wasn't really Jimmy up there, just some other flake.)

In this game Carew had four hits. In his last at-bat, in the eighth, he homered, raising his average to .403. He received one of the longest ovations I've ever seen at the Met. This was definitely Carew's greatest season. He flirted with a .400 average much of the year, and his picture was on the cover of *Sports Illustrated* with Ted Williams, who was the last player to hit .400 in a season, in 1941. Rod finished at .388, leading the league, and he set a new team record with 128 runs scored. And he had 100 RBIs for the first time in his career. He was the third Twin, after Killebrew and Versalles, to win the American League Most Valuable Player Award.

Even though Bill Campbell had signed with the Red Sox as a free agent, the Twins still had a pretty good bullpen in 1977, bolstered by a couple of Minnesota natives, Tommy Burgmeier and Tom Johnson. Dave Goltz, another Minnesotan—he was born in Pelican Rapids and grew up in the west-central part of the state—won 20 games. Dave was as reliable and steady as they come. His best pitch was a knuckle-curveball, and his delivery, especially his stride, was remarkable. A lot of players talked about how lightly he landed on his front foot, so that after he pitched you couldn't see any evidence of where his foot had landed in front of the pitching rubber.

The free agent bug bit the Twins again. At the end of the 1977 season Larry Hisle signed with the Brewers, and Lyman Bostock, who had finished second to Carew in the batting race with a .336 average, went to the Angels. Nowadays players have to be in the majors a certain number of years before becoming a free agent, but in the early years of free agency, before all the details had been worked out in a bargaining contract between the players and owners, some very young players like Lyman Bostock were able to play out their options and sign elsewhere.

Lyman was a very nice young man and an outstanding hitter. It was so sad what happened with him. Near the end of the 1978 season, when the Angels were in Chicago for a series, Lyman was riding in a car in nearby Gary, Indiana, when he was shot to death by someone in another car. I remember the shock in the Twins clubhouse when we got the news. We were in Milwaukee at the time, and it was definitely tough on the guys when they heard what had happened to their friend and former teammate.

It was such a senseless thing and was a result of Lyman, through no fault of his own, being in the wrong place at the wrong time. When you think about it, if he hadn't left the Twins, he'd probably be alive today because he wouldn't have been at that spot at that time in Gary, Indiana.

In 1978 the Twins acquired Willie Norwood, Hosken Powell, and Jesus "Bombo" Rivera, all unknowns. "We lost Hisle and Bostock," a disappointed fan said sarcastically, "but don't worry—we've got Hosken and Bombo." None of these players measured up to those who had left, but Bombo Rivera was popular. Promoted as a write-in candidate at the University of Minnesota for student president, Bombo came in second in the election.

During the 1978 season, Griffith—quite reluctantly—signed reliever Mike Marshall. Marshall had won the Cy Young Award with the Dodgers in 1974, when he appeared in 106 games, an incredible total for a pitcher. But he also had a reputation as a troublemaker, and Calvin didn't know if he wanted to mess with him. Mauch, however, was very adamant about wanting Marshall and reportedly threatened to resign if Calvin didn't sign him. Marshall had pitched for Mauch with the Montreal Expos, and Gene figured he knew him well enough that he wouldn't create any problems on the club. Calvin finally gave in and signed Marshall, who had a pretty good season, saving 21 games even though he didn't join the team until mid-May.

It wasn't much of a year for the Twins. They won only 73 games and finished fourth, 19 games out of first.

I had a different partner for a couple of years starting in 1978. Frank Quilici left to pursue some business interests, and he was replaced by Joe McConnell. Joe was primarily a football announcer—he did Vikings' games for many years—and brought a high-decibel style to the Twins. Like Larry Calton, he became excited about every play, although he didn't rub so many people the wrong way. But Joe sometimes irritated Gene Mauch by criticizing his tactics. Once Mauch pulled the infield in to be ready to cut off a run at the plate. Joe said, "Here we go, making a .400 hitter out of a .220 hitter." Joe was a hard worker, though, and did his homework, sometimes too much perhaps. If he knew the rotation scheduled for the next few games, he'd make out his scorecard in advance and then get upset if Mauch changed his lineup. McConnell should have been with us in 1962, when Mele went with the same lineup almost every day.

Frank Quilici returned to the booth in 1980 and was my partner for three more years. We enjoyed working together and had a lot of fun on the road. Frank had many friends

160

wherever we went; almost anything you needed, Frank could get it for you wholesale. He got me some suits at very good prices. Frank was from Chicago, and his parents visited us in the press box at Comiskey Park. Frank's folks made great Polish sausage and brought some for us, but we usually had just eaten dinner, and they never understood why we couldn't eat three Polish sausages each. Frank's dad has passed on, but his mother still lives in the same old house in Chicago. Frank has encouraged her to move, but she has too many friends and bingo parties to leave.

The free-agent specter still haunted Minnesota in 1978. Rod Carew, winning his seventh batting title, was on the last year of his contract. At that time a player had to play out an option year after his contract expired to become a free agent, so Carew would become a free agent after the 1979 season. Griffith decided to trade him after the 1978 season, rather than lose him without getting anyone in return, as had happened with Campbell, Hisle, and Bostock. As a ten-and-five man (ten years in the league and five years with the same team), Carew had the right to veto any trade, and he rejected Griffith's proposed trade to the Giants for Mike Ivie and a few other players. Instead, Rod went to the Angels in exchange for several players, the best being outfielder Ken Landreaux, who in 1979 had a .305 batting average with 15 home runs and 83 RBIs. To replace Carew at first, Griffith acquired first baseman Ron Jackson in another trade with the Angels, for Danny Ford. Jackson's nickname was Papa Jack, but his performance with the Twins prompted St. Paul sportswriter Pat Reusse to dub him Poppa Up.

As the 1979 season opened, a debate was raging over where the Twins would play in the future. Ever since his long-term lease at Met Stadium had expired after the 1975 season, Griffith had been operating on a year-by-year lease. He had made it clear he would not sign another long-term lease unless the Met was substantially improved or a new stadium was built. In late 1978 the commission had decided on a new domed stadium for downtown Minneapolis, but the public opposition was vociferous. Meanwhile, on the field the Twins had a good team and stayed in the race until the final week of the 1979 season and drew a million fans to the Met.

Mike Marshall led the league with 32 saves and appeared in 90 games, which is still an American League record. Marshall still also holds the National League record with 106 appearances with the Dodgers in 1974, when he pitched a total of 208 innings, all in relief, as much as a lot of starters throw these days. Marshall excelled in pickoff throws to first base and had an excellent screwball. He received his doctorate in kinesiology and claimed that a pitcher who followed the proper mechanics would never have a sore arm.

During the off-season, the Twins had acquired Jerry Koosman—who had grown up near Morris, Minnesota—from the Mets. In 1979, his first year with the Twins, Jerry won 20 games. I remember one game against the Royals. He pitched a great game even though he didn't know he was going to be pitching that night. There was an injury to one of the other starters and Jerry was called on unexpectedly. What a game he pitched even though he told me later he didn't think he would last more than three or four innings since he had spent the day clearing brush off the land near his house and was pretty tired when he got to the stadium.

Apparently, fatigue agreed with Koos that night. He had a perfect game into the sixth before giving up a home run to John Wathan. That was the only baserunner off him until Willie Wilson singled with two out in the ninth. Koosman was a real throwback to the old school, pitching a two-hitter on such short notice.

Jerry won number 20 in the final game of the season. Not

only that, he shutout the Milwaukee Brewers. It was the first time all season the Brewers had been held scoreless, and, if not for Koosman, they would have become the only team other than the 1932 Yankees to go an entire season without being shutout. (Koosman, like Marshall, had a great pickoff move. He picked off 15 runners in 1979, which I believe is still a league record.)

Another great addition in 1979 was rookie John Castino at third base. John tied with shortstop Alfredo Griffin of the Toronto Blue Jays as the American League Rookie of the Year. Gene Mauch used to say that Castino was the Twins' best athlete, able to play almost any position very well if necessary. A few years later John moved to second base and was outstanding there. Unfortunately, back problems put a premature end to his career.

Roy Smalley also had a great year. He cooled off a bit in the second half of the season, but he still ended up with 24 home runs and 95 runs batted in.

The Twins finished 1979 with an 82-80 record, only four games out of first place, despite losing six of their last seven games. That was the last full year for Gene Mauch as manager.

In late August 1980 Gene Mauch resigned when the Twins were in fourth place, wallowing with a record of 54-71. The Twins had finished fourth the last three years, but this time they were 26½ games out of first place and 17 games under .500. Gene Mauch was a stickler for knowing the rules, an intense manager who rewarded dumb plays on the field with a devastating frown. In his almost four years as manager, I learned a lot about the game from him in our many breakfasts together when the team was on the road. He later had some good years managing the California Angels and won a couple of division titles, although he never made it to the World Series. In 1995 Gene became a coach with the Kansas City Royals. He was back in uniform, on the field, right where he should be.

After Mauch resigned as Twins' manager in August 1980, he was replaced by coach Johnny Goryl, who, like Gene, had played for both the Minneapolis Millers and the St. Paul Saints. Goryl was also a former Twins' player. The Twins caught fire the rest of the season and won 23 of 36 games, including a 12-game winning streak.

During the 1980 season Ken Landreaux hit in 31-straight games, still a team record. That year the player with the longest hitting streak in the majors was to receive a gift from one of baseball's big sponsors, but before the season was over, Commissioner Bowie Kuhn ruled that such a gift wasn't proper. By this time, it was apparent that Landreaux would have the longest hitting streak, and he made it known he was very unhappy about it all. He ended up sulking and slumped toward the end of the year.

Landreaux had a sweet swing. In the second home game of the 1980 season, he hit a ninth-inning double to break up a no-hit bid by Bruce Kison of the California Angels. If not for that hit by Landreaux, the game would have set a record for the most lopsided no-hit win ever, since the Angels won 17-0. Someone asked me about this type of situation. The Twins had no chance of winning, so did I find myself pulling for the opposing pitcher to complete his no hitter? Let me put it this way. If I were a player and my team had no hits, I'd want to get a hit to break it up. And even as an announcer, I don't want to see my team get no-hit. So even though the Twins were hopelessly out of it, I was still happy to see Landreaux get that double and break up the no-hitter.

Ken Landreaux was a good hitter and a pretty good outfielder, but he often seemed morose and preoccupied, as if he didn't have his head in the game. At the end of the 1980 season the Twins traded him to the Dodgers for Mickey Hatcher.

Because of the Twins' improved performance under him in 1980, Johnny Goryl was offered the managing position for 1981. John had always been a hard-nosed, bear-down player, a fine utility player, but off the field he was very easy-going and just liked being one of the guys, so one day in Milwaukee near the end of the season he told me he was undecided about taking the manager's job and asked for my opinion. "If you're going to make baseball a career," I said, "you have to give it a shot because you may never get a chance to manage in the big leagues again."

John accepted the job for 1981, but the Twins won only 11 of their first 36 games. In May Griffith replaced Goryl with another coach, Billy Gardner, who, like John, was a former player with both the Minnesota Twins and the Minneapolis Millers. I had known Gardner when he played for the Baltimore Orioles in the 1950s.

The 1981 season certainly was best known for its mid-season strike. This one was the longest to date, lasting 50 days, which, unfortunately, was still shorter than the strike that began in 1994 and lasted until almost the end of April 1995.

The issue surrounding the 1981 dispute was the owners wanting a player, rather than merely an amateur draft choice, in return for a player they lost to free agency. The season was interrupted in mid-June and didn't resume until almost the middle of August.

During the strike Frank Quilici and I followed play-by-play records and re-created some big games, including the 1969 game in which Rich Reese hit a grand slam to snap Dave McNally's winning streak. Frank had played in that game and had hit one of the singles that set up the grand slam, and now he was pretending to announce it.

165

When the strike was settled, the owners designed a split-season format. All the teams who were in first place when the strike began were declared the first-half winners, and they would take on the second-half winners in the division playoffs. The Twins had a terrible season, finishing at 41-68 overall, but they played better in the second half, finishing with a 24-29 record after having gone 17-39 in the first half, and they were in contention until the final week.

The second half season introduced some new Twins who would form the nucleus of the team that would win the World Series six years later. Kent Hrbek and Tim Laudner, both Minnesota natives, and Gary Gaetti each broke in with a home run in his first game in the majors. On August 24 at Yankee Stadium, facing George Frazier with the game tied in the twelfth, Herbie hit a game-winning home run into the right-field seats. At Texas a month later Gaetti, in his first at-bat, hit a homer off knuckleballer Charlie Hough.

The 1981 season was the last at Metropolitan Stadium, which a visiting writer once called a "Fortress on the Prairie." The Twins were scheduled to open the next season in the new Hubert H. Humphrey Metrodome in downtown Minneapolis. In 1981, the last season the Met Stadium, the Twins drew only 469,090 fans. They lost dates because of the strike, of course, but their average of 7,951 fans per game was even less than their previous low in 1974, the year Larry Calton said he'd help them draw a million. On September 30, a Wednesday afternoon, in the last baseball game played at the Met, the Twins lost, 5-2, to the Kansas City Royals. Roy Smalley was the last batter, popping out to shortstop U. L. Washington. This game clinched a play-off spot for the Royals and eliminated the Twins from the pennant race. For many fans the end of Metropolitan Stadium was like losing a friend.

A Whole New Ball Game

Leaving the grass field of Metropolitan Stadium for the artificial turf of the Metrodome meant that the Twins needed some players with speed. They also needed additional pitching. So in January 1982 the Twins traded a couple of minor-leaguers for Dodgers' center fielder Bobby Mitchell, a good young prospect, and right-handed pitcher Bobby Castillo. Castillo's best pitch was a screwball, which he had taught to Fernando Valenzuela, who in 1981 had received both the Cy Young and the Rookie of the Year awards.

The three players—Hrbek, Laudner, and Gaetti—who had broken in with home runs in 1981 were a key part of the team. This trio was joined by another fine young player, Tom Brunansky, in May in one of several controversial trades Calvin Griffith made early in the season. He probably drew the most heat for the trade of Doug Corbett and Rob Wilfong for Brunansky, but this certainly turned out to be a good deal in the long run. Corbett had done a good job in relief for the Twins for a couple of seasons but never did much after leaving the Twins.

The other two trades were with the Yankees and involved the departure of Roy Smalley and Butch Wynegar. Smalley, it was felt, had slowed down a little bit and would not be nearly as effective on an artificial surface as he had been on natural grass. Griffith was blasted for these deals, as well, but one of the trades brought the Twins Greg Gagne, who didn't play for them right away but went on to become the most dependable shortstop they've ever had. That same deal also brought them Ron Davis, an unforgettable figure and a much-booed but also much-loved player. Ron was a very hyper guy on the mound. Once in Boston he was so nervous that he didn't wait for a sign from catcher Mark Salas but threw a pitch before Salas had put his mask on.

I got to know "R. D." pretty well, since he purchased a house not far from where we live. As a matter of fact, his house was probably no more than 250 yards from ours, although it was on a different street. I could look out our dining room window and see the Davis' house. But to drive between the two places, you had to go about a mile because there was no through street between them. One day Ron and his wife, Millie, had driven over to our house. Ron looked out our dining room window and said, "Hey, Hon [hopefully referring to Millie and not me], I thought the builder told us there wasn't another house like ours in this area. Look down there. There's one just like ours." I had a hard time convincing Ron that it was his house.

The Twins opened the dome in 1982 with a couple of exhibition games against the Philadelphia Phillies. It was fitting that the Phillies' Pete Rose got the first hit in the new stadium. Kent Hrbek had the first home run in that same game, a long shot off the facing of the upper deck in right. He hit another one later in the game off Sparky Lyle.

A few nights later in the first inning of the Metrodome's first regular-season game, against the Seattle Mariners, the Twins' Dave Engle, one of the players received from California in exchange for Rod Carew, hit the first regular-season home run, also the first hit, off Seattle's Floyd Bannister. Gary Gaetti hit two homers and just missed a third when he was thrown out at the plate trying for an inside-the-park home run. Pete Redfern, with the Twins since 1976, threw the Metrodome's first pitches in both the first exhibition and the regular-season games. The 1982 season would be Pete's last. He had some tough luck after his baseball days were over. He broke his neck in a diving accident and was paralyzed.

The Twins' attendance, helped by the big opening-night crowd, improved considerably, but they failed to draw a million fans and ended up last in attendance in the majors. The dome didn't have air conditioning that first year. Instead, huge fans in the Metrodome walls were designed to draw in cool air from outside. But in the summer in the Twin Cities it's warm until the sun sets around 9:30 or so. In August we had a heat wave for ten days, and many fans left the games early. After pitching a day game in there Jack Morris of the Tigers said he had never been so warm and uncomfortable in his life. Another problem the Twins had with the Metrodome was the fact that sightlines in the stadium were designed for football. The main pressure for a new park had come from the Minnesota Vikings, because Met Stadium had not been good for football, especially with the smallest seating capacity in the National Football League. Hence the Metrodome's design tends to favor football.

In 1982 the Twins turned in the majors' worst record, at 60-102, the first time they had lost more than 100 games. Determined to improve in the second half of the season, the Twins set a goal of playing .500 ball the rest of the way, but then in the first game after the All-Star break, at home against Detroit, the Tigers scored 11 runs in the top of the first inning. Sportswriter Pat Reusse claims that one day late in the season as he arrived at the Metrodome, he struck up a conversation with a man accompanied by his two little boys. Pat mentioned how nice it was that he was taking his kids to see the Twins. The man replied, "Yeah, and if they don't start behaving, I'm going to bring them again tomorrow." Despite their bad record, the Twins gave the fans something to cheer about. Hrbek had a 23-game hitting streak early in the year and by June 10 had 15 home runs. He finished the year with 23 homers and 92 runs batted in. Left fielder Gary Ward, with the Twins since 1980, hit 28 home runs with 91 RBIs. Third baseman Gary Gaetti wasn't far behind with 25 home runs and 84 driven in. Bobby Castillo, with a record of 13-11, was the Twins' best pitcher in 1982, and Ron Davis turned in 22 saves. Beyond that, there wasn't much in the pitching department. Although Frank Viola joined the team during the season, and later became a great pitcher, he struggled as a rookie and had a record of 4-10.

When Bobby Mitchell, the regular center fielder, went into a slump in May, going 33 at-bats without a hit, Jim Eisenreich, a native of St. Cloud, Minnesota, took over center field. He played well, but he began to hyperventilate and twitch involuntarily. Once in Fenway Park the fans in the center-field bleachers ridiculed and mocked him. This condition ended the 1982 season early for Eisenreich. He was in the opening-day lineup for the Twins again in 1983 and 1984, but each year the disorder cut short his season. The Twins even hired the St. Paul hypnotist, Harvey Maisel, who had worked with some major-league teams, but his treatments didn't help, and Eisenreich had to retire from the game. His problem was finally diagnosed as Tourette's Syndrome, and medication controlled the spasms. Jim went on to a good career with the Kansas City Royals and Philadelphia Phillies.

Since Roy Smalley had been traded away early in the year, Ron Washington played most games at shortstop. Ron, who had started his career as a catcher, was a hustling ballplayer who hit .271, but his fielding was erratic. He was versatile, though better suited for a utility role.

John Castino did an outstanding job at second base, but he missed the last part of the 1982 season when he needed spinal fusion surgery. The back problems resurfaced in 1983, his last full season in baseball.

My partner Frank Quilici left again after the 1982 season to pursue other business interests, and my new partner in 1983 was Tim Moreland. He came from Nebraska, where he had announced Cornhusker football. Originally, he was hired to announce Vikings football, and he knew much more about football than baseball. Once there was a runner on first when the batter hit a line drive to right, and since the runner on first had to hold up in case it was caught, the right fielder forced that runner out at second.

On the air Tim said, "There's a base hit to right field." Then after the throw beat the runner to second, he said, "What do we have here, Herb?"

I said, "Tim, that's a plain old force out, right fielder to shortstop."

During the All-Star break, Moreland was replaced by Ron Weber, a hockey expert who understood baseball pretty well. He was from Washington, D. C., and had announced for the Washington Capitals. He prepared a lot of material for each game, especially data on "This day in baseball . . ." Since he couldn't save this material for the next game, he'd try to squeeze it in, perhaps talking a little too much. At the end of the season he was replaced by Joe Angel.

Despite the addition of air conditioning in the Metrodome in June of 1983 and even though the Twins improved their record to 70-92, they drew just 858,939 fans, down more than 60,000 from the year before when they had had the worst record in baseball. They ended up 29 games out of first place. The Twins had lost 64 more games than they had won in their first two years in the Metrodome. The improvement by ten games in the won-loss record in 1983 was due

171

mainly to the pitching of a comparative unknown, Ken Schrom, who had signed with the Twins in spring training but had not made the club when the season opened. He was called up early in the year, though, and started in the bullpen. When he performed well in long relief, Billy Gardner put him in the starting rotation, and Schrom had a season record of 15-8. Unfortunately, the big winner from the year before, Bobby Castillo, fell to 8-12. Frank Viola, in his second season, was 7-15. Frank still had not perfected his change-up, a pitch he was learning from coach Johnny Podres. The opening-day pitcher, right-hander Al Williams, a former Sandanista guerrilla in Nicaragua, posted a record of 11-14. The Twins definitely needed more pitchers, so in December 1983 they sent run-producing outfielder Gary Ward to the Rangers in exchange for two right-handed pitchers, Mike Smithson and John Butcher.

During the next winter there was speculation that the Twins might leave Minnesota. When Calvin Griffith signed a 30-year contract for the Twins to play in the Metrodome, he included an escape clause: if the Twins did not average 1.4 million fans per year in any three-year period, Griffith could be released from the contract. Since the Twins had totaled less than 1.8 million in their first two seasons combined, attendance would have to exceed 2.4 million in 1984 or Griffith could exercise that option. A group in Tampa, Florida, hoping to acquire the Twins and move the team to the Tampa Bay area, purchased the minority stockholdings of Gabe Murphy. A longtime member of the Twins' front office said to me, "If you want to keep announcing the Twins' games, you might think about putting your home up for sale, because it looks to me like we're going to be playing baseball in Tampa."

Meanwhile, groups within the Twin Cities' business community formed task forces to buy enough Twins tickets so that Calvin couldn't get out of his lease with the stadium commission. They gave some tickets to underprivileged kids, but most of the tickets they bought weren't used. The situation was a bit ludicrous at times. In May for a midweek afternoon game against Toronto the paid attendance was 52,000 even though only about 7,000 people actually went to the game. That year the Twins set a team record with attendance of nearly 1.6 million, although at least 150,000 of the tickets were sold through the buyout effort of the business community.

Of course, even that inflated figure of 1.6 million wouldn't have been enough to keep Griffith from escaping his lease, had he wanted to. But as it turned out, it didn't matter. During the course of the season, Calvin agreed to sell the club to banker Carl Pohlad.

Calvin was one of the last pure baseball owners in the game. Most other owners had many business interests and just owned a baseball team on the side, but Calvin had no source of income other than the Twins. Ever since the end of the reserve clause in 1975, the salaries of players had been skyrocketing, and Calvin could no longer match salaries for star players. So after 60 years in the game, starting out as a batboy, pitching and managing in the minors, and going all the way to owner, Cal Griffith transferred the Minnesota Twins to Carl Pohlad in a very emotional pregame ceremony on June 22, 1984.

At that time the Twins were three and a half games out of first place, and they continued to play well the rest of the way. With one week left in the season, the Twins were in first place. The Twins had seven games left, three in Chicago and four in Cleveland. They won the first game against the White Sox but then dropped the next two.

They were still in the race when they got to Cleveland but probably needed at least three wins to have any chance of winning the division. In the first game against the Indians the Twins had the lead with two out in the ninth and were on the verge of winning and moving to within a game of the first-place Kansas City Royals, when journeyman Jamie Quirk came out of the Cleveland dugout to pinch hit with runners aboard. Quirk connected for a home run off Ron Davis and turned a seemingly sure win into a crushing loss for the Twins.

Things got even worse the next night. The Twins, with Frank Viola pitching, built a 10-0 lead by the fifth inning. Then the Indians staged one of the great comebacks in baseball history and won the game, 11-10. Gary Gaetti made a key throwing error during one of the Indians' rallies. Never one to make excuses, he said after the game, "It's kind of hard to throw the ball when you have your hands around your throat," implying that he had choked on the play.

Despite the disappointing finish, the 1984 season was promising for the Twins, who finished just three back of the Royals. Kent Hrbek hit 27 home runs and drove in 107 runs, becoming the first Twin to knock in at least 100 runs since Hisle and Carew both turned the trick in 1977. In the league MVP voting, Hrbek came in second to Tiger reliever Willie Hernandez. In his third season Frank Viola emerged as the Twins' top starter, with an 18-12 record.

In May 1984 the Twins called up Kirby Puckett to replace outfielder Jim Eisenreich, who was retiring because of his nervous disorder. Kirby had been playing for the Twins' Triple-A club, the Toledo Mud Hens, in the International League, and when he got the call to the majors, the Mud Hens were playing in Portland, Maine, while the Twins were in Anaheim, California. After his cross-country flight Kirby got a cab at the airport terminal, and told the driver to take him to Anaheim Stadium, not realizing it was 50 miles away. The fare was around $75. Kirby didn't have enough money, so the Twins' traveling secretary took care of the bill. All the travel and turmoil might have been upsetting to some, but Kirby must have been able to take it in stride. After all, the next night he broke into the majors with four hits in his first game.

Kirby was a quiet guy when he first got to the majors, but he grew into the role of leader. And as he became more comfortable with his teammates, he became a lot more outgoing. He's one of those guys who never seems to be in a bad mood. He can really liven up a clubhouse, especially by poking fun at himself. Kirby is always ubpeat and always a pleasure to be around.

About a month after Puckett joined the Twins, the Metrodome came in for more criticism in a game at home against the White Sox. Chicago right-hander Richard Dotson carried a 2-0 lead into the last of the ninth. The Twins had a couple of runners aboard with one out when Tim Teufel dropped a base hit into short right field. As right-fielder Harold Baines trotted in to field the hit, the ball apparently hit a seam in the artificial turf, bounced over his head, and rolled all the way to the right-field fence. By the time the White Sox chased the ball down and relayed it in, Teufel was sliding home with a game-winning, three-run, inside-the-park home run on a fluke fly ball. The Twins fans were delighted, but the White Sox manager, Tony LaRussa, criticized the playing surface at the Metrodome and said the play was a "disgrace to baseball."

Perhaps so, but I know from experience that these things don't just happen on synthetic turf. In fact, I'll bet Twins' manager Billy Gardner might have been reminded of this same play after watching Teufel's strange home run. When I was broadcasting for the Baltimore Orioles, I remember a 1959 game at home against, again in this case, the Chicago White Sox. The Baltimore pitcher, Billy O'Dell, came up to bat with Billy Gardner on base. O'Dell hit a high fly ball down the right-field line. Al Smith of the White Sox charged in, hoping to catch the ball, then finally backed off and decided to play in on the bounce. In those days, they had wood strips painted white for the foul lines in the outfield. O'Dell's fly ball came down right on the wooden foul line, bounced over Al Smith's head, and rolled all the way to the fence. Before he could retrieve it, Gardner and O'Dell had circled the bases. The inside-the-park home run put the Orioles' ahead, a game in which O'Dell eventually got the victory.

Despite his outstanding season, Hrbek, who had been a member of the American League All-Star team in 1982, did not make the All-Star team in 1984. Herbie was obviously upset by it and made the comment that he wouldn't play in any future All-Star games, even if he were voted in by the fans or chosen by the American League manager. Hrbek certainly hit well for the Twins over the years, and I've never seen a better fielding first baseman than Hrbek in his prime.

Joe Angel, who became my broadcast partner in 1984, liked to sometimes do a little managing from the broadcasting booth, and once in a while some of his attempts at humor didn't go over well with Midwestern listeners. Once at Yankee Stadium the message board announced that the next night would be Latin American Night. Joe read the message on the air and added, "I wonder what they're going to give away for Latin American Night—hubcaps?" On another occasion he read some information on a pitcher from Jamaica, New York. Joe said, "Jamaica? No, just shook hands." Joe spent three years as a Twins announcer and has since broadcast for the Orioles, Yankees, and Marlins. Overall, he worked at his job and was a good announcer.

In 1985 the Twins reacquired two of their former players. Before the season started, in February, the Twins got Roy

Smalley back in a trade. Ever since they had traded him away to the Yankees nearly three years before, they had never found anyone satisfactory for shortstop. One of the shortstops the Twins had tried was Alfonso "Houston" Jimenez, who was about five foot five. Once before a game I was standing by the batting cage with manager Billy Gardner, when Houston ran out to his position. Billy spat some tobacco juice and said, "There's our new shortstop. Hope we don't get too many high hops." Then in August 1985 the Twins got Bert Blyleven from Cleveland in exchange for four players, the best of whom was Jay Bell, who would eventually establish himself as a solid shortstop with the Pittsburgh Pirates. And speaking of former players, in 1985 Rod Carew, playing for the Angels, collected his 3,000th hit, off Frank Viola in a game against the Twins on a Sunday afternoon at Anaheim Stadium. I wanted to get Rod to sign my scorecard after the game, but it was a getaway game for us, and I didn't have a chance then. Fortunately, the Angels were coming to Minnesota a few days later, and he signed it then.

Hopes were high that the Twins, after flirting with first place in the Western Division for most of 1984, would be another strong contender in 1985, but in June the Twins had a 27-35 record, and Billy Gardner was fired.

I always enjoyed being around Billy Gardner, a blue-collar kind of guy. His family lived back in Connecticut, and during the season Billy rented a room at the Super 8 motel in Roseville, a few miles from the Metrodome.

Somebody asked him once, "Billy, you're a big-league manager, you're making good money, so what are you staying at a budget motel for?"

Billy said, "Well, I like it there. They're real nice to me. They even put me on the opposite side of the motel from where they park the 18-wheelers."

The new manager was Ray Miller, a highly regarded pitching coach with the Baltimore Orioles. The Twins played .500 ball the rest of the season, winning 50 and losing 50, and tied for fourth place in the Western Division, 14 games out of first place.

In 1985 the Twins hosted the All-Star Game for the second time. The Twins had only one player on the team, Tom Brunansky, who didn't even start and came to the plate just once. The National League won the game, 6-1, and I had the pleasure of presenting the All-Star MVP award to the winning pitcher, LaMarr Hoyt of the San Diego Padres.

Reliever Ron Davis got off to a slow start in 1985. In May the Twins had a four-game streak of allowing a ninth-inning home run to the opposition. The last one was a real crusher. They had a two-run lead over the Yankees in New York with two out, when Don Mattingly hit a three-run homer off Davis, winning for the Yankees. Three days later, pitching in a Thursday afternoon game at the Metrodome against the Tigers, Davis received an ovation from the fans, some of whom were wearing "I Believe in R. D." T-shirts. Ron got the save in that game and blew only one save in the rest of the season. The Twins played the song "Eye of the Tiger" when Davis came into a game. It seemed to pump him up a bit, although he was a pretty hyper guy anyway. Davis was a fan favorite for a while, but he was traded the following season. Ray Miller objected to Davis' inconsistency and his penchant for throwing a gopher ball, and during the off-season Miller persistently asked the front office to trade Davis for another reliever. But Davis managed to hang on in Minnesota until August 1986, a month before Miller also departed.

Before and during the 1986 season the Twins made seven separate trades and acquired 15 new players, 11 of whom were pitchers, including lefty Neal Heaton and right-hander

George Frazier. But all the dealing didn't have much effect on the won-lost record. The Twins had a poorer record in 1986, winning 71 and losing 91. Miller was fired in September, when the team had a record of 59-80. It was a tough blow for Ray, who felt he did not get a fair opportunity. Miller steadfastly maintained that the Twins could have turned many of those games around if they had had a stronger bullpen. Ray was replaced by coach Tom Kelly, who won 12 of the 23 games he managed.

Near the end of the 1986 season Bert Blyleven set a major-league record when he gave up his 50th home run of the season. The player who hit it was Jay Bell, one of the players traded by the Twins to get Blyleven. Bell hit the record-breaking home run on the first pitch delivered to him in the majors. As Bell circled the bases and it was announced that Blyleven had set the record for the most home runs allowed in a season, Bert smiled and tipped his hat to the fans.

Ray Miller had been right: the Twins needed a better bullpen. After the 1986 season the Twins designated Mark Portugal, a young right-hander, as their bullpen ace. Portugal had not yet matured as a pitcher, but he had a great arm and probably had as much stuff as anyone on the staff. But then the Twins traded Neal Heaton to the Montreal Expos in exchange for reliever Jeff Reardon.

There was more excitement when free-agent Jack Morris, a St. Paul native who had been one of the league's top pitchers in recent years with the Tigers, came to Minnesota for contract talks. Nothing came of the meeting, however. The Twins said Morris had made contract demands they were unwilling to meet. Even though Morris was possibly the best free-agent pitcher available, he wasn't getting any offers, and neither were some other outstanding free agents like Bob Horner and Tim Raines. In fact, few free agents of any value were getting contract offers from teams other than the ones they had just been playing for. What was going on was called collusion, and the owners would eventually pay dearly for it.

The Twins were also searching for a manager. Jim Frey became the front-runner, but he accepted a front-office job with the Cubs instead. When they couldn't sign Frey, the Twins decided to give Tom Kelly the job for 1987. He had played in the organization, coached, and served as the interim manager. They were about to offer Kelly $105,000 to manage the team in 1987, but since Tom Trebelhorn of the Brewers was getting only $100,000, that's the amount they offered Kelly. Tom may have felt put off by the process, but he accepted the offer. T.K. just wanted a chance to prove he could manage in the majors.

The Magic Season

In 1987 the Twins switched back to uniforms with pin-stripes, red this time instead of navy blue and with a new logo and lettering. There was a change in broadcast partners, too. Joe Angel was replaced by John Rooney and John Gordon. John Rooney started with television but did some radio from time to time, but eventually Rooney announced only on television, and John Gordon was my regular partner on radio. And Gordo's been with me ever since. John had been with the Baltimore Orioles and then the Yankees, and he'd announced football and basketball for the University of Virginia.

The Twins won their season opener at the Metrodome against the A's. The game was tied in the top of the tenth when Mickey Tettleton of Oakland hit a long fly to center. It looked like a homer, but Kirby Puckett planted himself in front of the fence, leaped high, and caught the ball above the top of the fence. The Twins then won the game in the last of the tenth on a run-scoring single by Kent Hrbek. Two days later the Twins completed a sweep of Oakland as Dan Gladden singled in two runs in the last of the ninth for a 5-4 win. Danny had come to the Twins only about a week before, in a five-player deal with the San Francisco Giants. Playing left field and hitting lead-off, Gladden provided a lot of spark to the team. His nickname was "Gladwrench," but most of the players called him "Wrench."

The Twins played well through April but struggled during the first half of May. On May 14 they got drubbed by Toronto, 16-4, a loss that dropped them to .500 and four games out of first. The Twins got a lift in early June in a Saturday night game at home against Texas. After losing three in a row the Twins seemed on the verge of another loss as they trailed by a run in the last of the ninth. But then Mark Salas, a reserve catcher, blasted a pinch-hit homer and tied the game. The Twins eventually won in the 13th inning. Oddly enough, Salas hit that home run after the Twins had traded him to the New York Yankees: the Twins had worked out the deal during the game but would not announce it until the game was over.

In exchange for Salas, the Twins acquired knuckleballer Joe Niekro from the Yankees. Niekro had a reputation for illegally scuffing up baseballs to get a little more movement on his pitches, and when he was pitching in a game in California against the Angels, the umpiring crew decided to see if Niekro had anything on him that he could use to scuff a baseball. Joe pulled his back pockets inside out to show they were empty. In the process, however, something flew out from a pocket and landed in the infield grass. I saw it, the television cameras registered it, and the umpires saw it and picked it up. It was an emery board. Niekro was immediately ejected and subsequently suspended.

The next day Phil Niekro, Joe's brother and an outstanding knuckleballer himself, sent Joe an electric sander. The following week Joe was a guest on David Letterman's late-night show, because the television replay of his attempt to discard the emery board had made highlight shows across the country. Joe showed up on Letterman's set wearing a utility belt loaded with tools that could be used to scuff a baseball.

Around this time the Twins acquired veteran southpaw

Steve Carlton, who had won the Cy Young Award four times while pitching for the Philadelphia Phillies and had 328 career wins at the time he joined the Twins. He got only one more win after that, though, when he nearly shut out the Oakland A's at the Metrodome in early August. Carlton's best days were behind him, and although he finished the season and pitched again for the Twins before retiring a month into the next season, Lefty wasn't even eligible to be part of the postseason roster in 1987.

Teams are required to set their rosters for the playoffs and the World Series on the first of September. After that, they can expand their rosters only by calling up minor-leaguers. The Twins dropped Carlton off the roster on August 31 but then put him back on the next day. The player they added in between that time, making him eligible for the playoffs, was Don Baylor, a veteran outfielder and designated hitter and a former American League Most Valuable Player. The Twins acquired him from the Red Sox to give them an extra right-handed bat and also for leadership. Baylor had been through pennant races before, and that experience could rub off on some of the younger players.

The Twins were really getting it together as they entered September and the stretch drive. Their front-line pitchers, Frank Viola and Bert Blyleven, were steady, as were the pitchers in the bullpen, especially closer Jeff Reardon. Kent Hrbek was the team's best hitter, finishing with 34 homers, but Kirby Puckett was spectacular, too, particularly in the final month. At the end of August in a game at Milwaukee, Puckett had six hits, including two homers and two doubles. On September 3 at the Metrodome, when the Twins were down by a run to Boston with two out in ninth, Puckett drilled a frozen rope into the left-field seats tying the game. I have rarely seen a ball leave the playing field that quickly. The Twins won the game in extra innings.

The Twins were pulling away from Oakland and Kansas City in September. Their final home game of the season, against the Royals on a Sunday afternoon, drew a full house, putting the season's attendance total over two million for the first time in the history of the Twins. Kansas City had won the first two games of the series and was threatening in the top of the first inning in this final game, with speedy Willie Wilson on third and another runner on first and no outs. George Brett grounded into a force at second, but instead of relaying to first for the double play, Al Newman, the second baseman, fired home to nail Wilson trying to score from third. The Twins then exploded with a big inning in the last of the first and cruised to an easy win.

Minnesota's magic number was now one: they had at least a tie for the division title, with a week still left in the season. The clincher came the next night in Texas, as the Twins beat the Rangers.

After the game I said to third baseman Gary Gaetti, "It's too bad we couldn't have clinched at home."

"No," he replied, "we wanted to do it here so we could trash their field."

The Twins closed the regular season the following Sunday, finishing with a record of 85-77, eight games over .500. All seven teams of the Western Division were pretty evenly matched, and only ten games separated the best from the worst, whereas the Eastern Division had a couple of very good teams, Toronto and Detroit, and a couple of very bad teams, Cleveland and Baltimore. The Twins gave up 20 runs more than they scored during the season, and they struggled all year on the road, but they won when they had to and were especially tough in the Metrodome, which paid off in the post-season when they had the home-field advantage in both the league playoffs and the World Series.

Their opponents in the American League playoffs were

the Detroit Tigers, who had won 98 games during the regular season, 13 more than the Twins, so the Tigers were heavy favorites to win the playoffs.

Before the playoffs started, Brent Musburger of CBS Television asked me, "Do you think the Twins have any kind of chance against the Tigers?"

"Shoot, yes," I said, "we're going to win."

The Twins finished off the Tigers in five games, the first two at home, then two out of three at Tiger Stadium.

The final game was on Monday afternoon in Detroit. As we boarded the plane for the flight to Minnesota, we heard that the Metrodome would be open that night for a rally to let fans greet the American League champions. During the flight the captain announced that people were already arriving at the Metrodome, and perhaps 25,000 fans would be there by the time we arrived. They guessed low. Fans filled the Metrodome, and many more couldn't get in. When we walked onto the field and saw all those people, some of the guys, including Gary Gaetti, were in tears.

The National League playoffs were still going on. The San Francisco Giants led their playoff series three games to two, but the Cardinals took the last two and won the pennant.

Minnesota and St. Louis were well matched and the Twins appeared to be in pretty good shape going into the series. If it went the limit, to seven games, they could get three starts out of Frank Viola and two from Bert Blyleven. Also, St. Louis was hampered by injuries. Jack Clark, who had had a fantastic season with the bat, had a problem with his leg and had to be replaced on the World Series roster. And Terry Pendleton, a switch-hitter, had a pulled muscle that didn't allow him to hit right-handed. He would have to swing left-handed against a left-handed pitcher or else not hit at all against southpaws. Furthermore, the Twins had the home-field advantage again: they would open with two at the Metrodome and would have the final two there if the series went that long. And was that Metrodome noisy. For once I wore a headset on the air just to block out the noise.

The Twins gave their fans plenty to cheer about in the first two games, as Viola and Blyleven each picked up a win. Dan Gladden broke open the first game with a grand slam. In St. Louis the Cardinals won three in a row, to taking a 3-2 series lead.

The sixth game was on a Saturday afternoon at the Metrodome with John Tudor, the Cardinals' fine left-hander, on the mound. St. Louis built a 5-2 lead into the last of the fifth inning, and if Tudor could go a couple more innings, the Cards could get into their bullpen, which had been tough all year. The Twins had to do something quick. They did.

Puckett opened with a single, and Gaetti followed with a run-scoring double. Then Don Baylor lifted a two-run homer to left field, tying the game. The Metrodome went wild. Before they were done in the fifth, the Twins picked up another run, taking a 6-5 lead. In the next inning the Twins loaded the bases, with two out. Kent Hrbek was coming up, so the Cardinal skipper, Whitey Herzog, brought in Ken Dayley, a left-hander. Herbie greeted him with a blast over the center-field fence, a grand slam that broke it open. There would be a seventh game.

So far the series had gone just as it had for the Twins in 1965: winning two at home, being swept on the road, and coming home to win the sixth game. The Twins hoped this one would have a different ending, though.

Viola was on the mound in Game Seven. The Cardinals built a 2-0 lead, but the Twins tied it, even though two runners were thrown out at the plate. The Twins took the lead in the last of the sixth on an infield hit by Greg Gagne, then added an insurance run in the eighth. Viola had pitched great, but it was left to Jeff Reardon to finish it off in the ninth. He retired the first two batters and then faced Willie McGee, who hit a grounder down to Gaetti at third. As Gary threw it across the diamond to Hrbek, I called out into my microphone, "And the Twins are World Champions!"

Despite all the celebration, including a parade through both downtowns after the World Series, I still look back fondly on the 1965 season. Even though they didn't win, it was a coming of age for a team. But, of course, 1987 was great, too.

There was quite a celebration after the Twins won the World Series in 1987. The scene was repeated in 1991. *Linda Schaefer.*

Déjà Vu

The Twins had an even better team in 1988 and won 90 games for the first time since 1970, but they couldn't overcome a slow start and finished second to Oakland. The Twins did set a league attendance record, however. In the final month of the season, with a chance of drawing three million fans, the Twins arranged some bulk sales of tickets, at greatly discounted prices, to various organizations, including WCCO Radio. These organizations then gave the tickets to worthy groups in the Twin Cities. I'm not sure how many of those tickets actually translated into people in the stands, but in the final game of the season, the Twins went over three million in attendance. Even aided by a buyout, it was quite an accomplishment, especially considering that just a few years before the team had been on the verge of leaving because of a lack of fan support.

There were some great individual performances in 1988. Kirby Puckett had his best year ever, hitting .356 with 24 home runs and 121 RBIs. And Frank Viola had his best year ever, winning 24 games and becoming the second Twin to receive the Cy Young Award. Frank had a good arm when he first came up in 1982, but he couldn't control his emotions well. He eventually matured. And he turned the corner with his circle change-up, learned from Johnny Podres, the Twins' pitching coach in the 1980s. Frank would make a circle with his index finger and thumb, grip the ball with the other three fingers, and throw it with the same motion as for his fastball. Depending on how it left his hand, the ball acted like a screwball, breaking down and away from a right-handed batter, and the reduced speed threw off a hitter's timing.

Another Twins' left-hander, Allan Anderson, won the league's earned-run-average title although it was a bit controversial since he sat out his last start to protect his ERA. The next nearest pitcher, Teddy Higuera of Milwaukee, had made his final start of the year and still had an ERA a little higher than Anderson's. Rather than take the chance of getting hit hard, Anderson chose to take the day off and thereby received some heavy criticism.

Allan was a fine young man, and I think he was influenced by some of the veteran players. After all, sometimes a player hitting .300 sits out the last game of the season to protect that average. The classic example of doing it the other way is Ted Williams in 1941. Going into the last day of the season, when the Boston Red Sox were playing a double-header in Philadelphia, Williams' average was .3995, which, rounded off, would have put him at .400. No one had hit .400 since Bill Terry in 1930, and Williams could have protected his average by not playing, but that wasn't his style. He played both games, got six hits in eight at-bats, and finished with a .406 average. No one has hit .400 since.

In April 1988, when the team was struggling, the Twins traded Tom Brunansky to the St. Louis Cardinals for second baseman Tommy Herr. Bruno had been one of the "Fab Four," along with Hrbek, Gaetti, and Puckett, the heart of the team through the 1980s. But the Twins needed help at second base and thought that Herr, who had played against them in the World Series, might be the answer. As it turned out, he wasn't. Herr just didn't want to play in Minnesota. Afterward, Andy MacPhail, the Twins' vice president for baseball operations, said he would never again make a deal without checking whether the new player would be happy here.

An even more shocking trade took place at the end of July 1989. After his best season ever, Frank Viola, the league's reigning Cy Young award winner, got off to a pretty rocky start. Before the season opened, he and the Twins had been working on a contract extension, and when that fell through, the turmoil didn't help his pitching. He and the Twins finally reached terms on a new contract, but soon afterward the Twins traded him to New York for five pitchers, including Kevin Tapani and Rick Aguilera. Viola helped the Mets and later the Red Sox, and although his career was threatened by major surgery on his pitching arm, he made a comeback.

In 1989 Kirby Puckett became the first Twin since Rod Carew to win the American League batting title. Although Kirby didn't have as good a year as he'd had in 1988, he topped the league with a .337 batting average.

As a team, the Twins took a dip, finishing with an 80-82 record, their first losing season under Tom Kelly. Then in 1990 they dipped even further, finishing last, 29 games behind first-place Oakland.

The hopes weren't high for 1991, even though the Twins had some pretty good newcomers. After passing on the opportunity before the 1987 season, the Twins now signed Jack Morris, a St. Paul native. Morris wasn't as hot as he'd been a few years before, but he anchored the rotation, providing many innings pitched and a lot of leadership. The Twins also signed free agents Chili Davis, a switch-hitter with good power, and Mike Pagliarulo, a third baseman who had hit more than 30 home runs in a season shortly after coming up with the New York Yankees a few years before. But for some reason Pags wasn't a power hitter for the Twins; for

191

much of the 1991 season, Pagliarulo had fewer runs batted in than Davis had home runs. That also goes to show the impact Chili had on the team, giving them some strong hitting in the designated hitter slot.

The Twins had their best spring-training record ever, in a new home. As the Washington Senators and the Minnesota Twins, the team had trained at Tinker Field in Orlando since 1936, and their minor-league camp was in Jacksonville and later Melbourne, about 75 miles southeast of Orlando. The Twins had only one practice field other than the main diamond in Orlando, and the clubhouse there was very small and cramped.

Meanwhile, in Florida in the mid-1980s there had been a lot of competition in developing new spring-training sites. Many teams had switched locations: the Reds from Tampa to Plant City, the Rangers from Pompano Beach to Port Charlotte, and the Royals from Fort Myers to a location called Baseball City, at the junction of Interstate 4 and U.S. Highway 27, near Haines City, where I had gone to my first spring training with the Springfield Cubs in 1950. The Twins tried to work with the city of Orlando to make improvements or build a new stadium, but the most Orlando was willing to spend was two million, not enough to satisfy the Twins. Fort Myers, having lost the Royals, built the Twins the Lee County Sports Complex, a beautiful facility just south of the town. With four or five practice fields, the Twins have combined their minor-league and major-league training, so the managers and coaches now have an opportunity to see their farmhands.

When I started going to Orlando for spring training with the Twins in the early 1960s, Orlando had no other claim to fame. Not long after, the town grew with the construction of Disney World, but people were still excited to host the Twins every spring, and they were sorry when the Twins

Frank Quilici and I have always gotten along great and
felt very comfortable with one another during the years
we broadcast together. *WCCO Radio.*

John Gordon's been my partner with the Twins longer than anyone.
WCCO Radio.

Rod Carew signs my scorecard of the game in which he got his
3,000th hit as "Mudpie" looks on. *WCCO Radio.*

I joke around a little with manager Tom Kelly at a rally
right before the 1990 season opener.

Bob Allison and Harmon Killebrew, the heart and soul of the Twins'
batting order in the early 1960s. Bob died a couple weeks
before the 1995 season opened. *Linda Schaefer.*

moved to Fort Myers. Spring training was more relaxed at Orlando. The fans could show up anytime and find a pretty good seat, but now they have to buy tickets in advance. Fort Myers is less convenient for Kathy and me as well. A few years ago we bought a house just west of Orlando. At first we stayed there only during spring training, but eventually the house became our winter home, from late October until at the end of spring training. Now when training camp opens, we close up the home near Orlando and move to a condo in Fort Myers.

The new facilities clearly contributed to the Twins big improvement in 1991. For the first two months of that season, though, the Twins struggled. The opened the season in Oakland, where the A's Rickey Henderson was only three steals away from breaking Lou Brock's career record. In the final game of the series Junior Ortiz threw Henderson out at second in what would have been his record-tying steal. Henderson later left the game with a pulled hamstring, and nearly a month passed until he broke the record.

The Twins lost nine of their first 11, including a 15-9 loss at home against California in which the Angels' Dave Winfield hit three home runs. He had two more at bats after that and, while he didn't get his fourth homer of the night, he did end up with five hits and 15 total bases.

One of few the bright spots early in the season was Scott Erickson's pitching. Erickson pitched well but lost his first two games for lack of offensive support: the Twins were shut out in both games. But then he reeled off 12 wins in a row, from mid-April to nearly the end of June. Scott had a great sinking fastball and a hard slider, and batters just weren't hitting many balls hard off him. During his streak he was pitching about as well as I've ever seen over any length of time. He had a pair of back-to-back shutouts and almost made it three in a row in his next start, when he took a shutout into the ninth inning against the Red Sox at Fenway Park. Tom Brunansky, by this time with Boston, broke it up with a three-run homer, although Scott still got his fourth-straight win. The 12th game in his streak was a two-hit shutout on June 24 at Yankee Stadium. His winning streak was snapped in his next start: he carried a 3-2 lead into the seventh inning against Chicago, but the White Sox broke through for a five-run inning and won the game, Erickson's first loss in more than two months. Unfortunately, in this game Scott started feeling pain in his arm that bothered him for the rest of the season. He won 20 games that year, but he also spent some time on the disabled list and lost a chance to be the starting pitcher in the All-Star Game.

During the period of Erickson's hot pitching, there were a couple of other long streaks in the American League. The Texas Rangers were on fire in May when they won 14 games in a row. Their winning streak was snapped on May 28 by the Twins, who then started an even longer streak of their own a few days later. The Twins were 23-25 and in fifth place after a loss at Kansas City on Friday, May 31. The next day, against the Royals, Chili Davis hit a pair of two-run homers, each one breaking a tie, and the Twins won. On Sunday Erickson won his eighth-straight game and lowered his earned-run average to 1.58, the best in the American League. These two games were the start of a 15-game winning streak that put the Twins into first place in the American League West. It looked pretty good for 16 in a row in the opening of a series in Baltimore when the Twins held a two-run lead into the ninth. The Orioles scored one and had two runners on base with two out, as reliever Rick Aguilera faced the Orioles' Randy Milligan. Milligan doubled up the alley in left-center field, and two runs scored. The Orioles had stopped the Twins' streak.

Another pitcher was stepping up at this time: Jack Morris. He got hit pretty hard in his first few starts of the season, but then he found his form and became the team's stopper. The game that ended Scott Erickson's winning streak was the Twins' fourth loss in a row, but the next afternoon, Morris ended the slump with a six-hit shutout over the White Sox. It was Jack's eighth win in his last eight starts. He was the starter in the All-Star Game, which the American League won, 4-2, on a three-run homer by Baltimore's Cal Ripken. In the first inning of that game a line drive by Bobby Bonilla hit Morris in the ankle. The accident was reminiscent of Dizzy Dean's injury in the 1937 All-Star Game, when Earl Averill's line drive hit Dean on the toe. Dean tried to come back too soon after the injury. Favoring his sore toe, he altered his pitching delivery and developed a sore arm that eventually ended his career.

Morris was pitching again a few days after the All-Star Game, and a lot of people wondered if that was a wise thing. He looked good, however, in beating the Red Sox. He never did appear to have any ill effects from the incident in the All-Star Game and went on to win 18 games in the regular season.

Another Twins pitcher wasn't so lucky when he was hit by a batted ball. Denny Neagle, who had pitched at the University of Minnesota, made his major-league debut on July 27 in a game against the Brewers. He was pitching well, but in the fourth inning he was nailed on the elbow by a line drive and had to leave the game. Neagle went on the disabled list, and although he pitched later in the season, he was not on the postseason roster.

One of the Twins' biggest series that year was at the Metrodome in mid-August against the Oakland A's, who had been in the World Series the last three years and were now in third place, trailing the Twins by four games. In the opener of this four-game series, on a Friday night, Oakland had a 4-2 lead in the ninth inning with their outstanding reliever Dennis Eckersley on the mound, but the Twins rallied for two runs, tying the game, and then won in the twelfth on an infield single by Hrbek. In the Saturday game the Twins fell behind, 4-1, but then scored 11 runs and won, 12-4. On Sunday the A's led, 4-1, but the Twins scored two in the seventh and three in the eighth to win. It was Oakland's fifth loss in a row. On Monday night in the series finale, the Twins trailed by 6-1 and came back to tie the score. This time, however, the A's still came out on top, winning 8-7 on a run-scoring single by Terry Steinbach in the top of the ninth. Even though the A's won the last game, this series seemed to break Oakland's back. The Twins' main rival the rest of the way was the Chicago White Sox, although the Texas Rangers were playing well too.

Down the stretch drive, still another pitcher on the staff distinguished himself. Kevin Tapani won nine games in a row between late July and early September and finished the season with 16 wins.

On Saturday, September 28 in Toronto, Morris shut out the Blue Jays with six hits for his 18th win, reducing the Twins' magic number to one. They had clinched a tie for the title. On Sunday the Twins lost to the Blue Jays, but on the bus to the airport we heard that the White Sox, the only remaining contender, had also lost, so the Twins had the Western Division title.

The Twins faced the Blue Jays in the American League playoffs. The playoffs opened in the Metrodome, and the Twins and Blue Jays each won a game. The series now seemed to favor Toronto since they'd have the next three games at home, but the Twins swept the games at SkyDome and took the American League pennant.

The Atlanta Braves and the Pittsburgh Pirates were still

battling in the National League playoffs. The Braves finally won in the seventh game. That meant that the world champions of 1991 would be a team that had finished in last place the year before, something that had never before happened. I think the Twins were the better team, although the Braves were stronger than the Cardinals had been when the Twins won the 1987 World Series. The Braves were well balanced with good power and a terrific front line of starting pitchers in Tommy Glavine, John Smoltz, and Steve Avery.

Some have called this the best World Series ever. I wouldn't single out any one as the best, but the Twins and Braves fought as exciting a World Series as you could hope for. Five of the games were decided in a team's last at-bat. Three games, including the last two, went extra innings.

Morris pitched the opener, at the Metrodome, and won, 5-2. The second game, which featured a pitching matchup of Kevin Tapani and Tom Glavine, was tied, 2-2, until Scott Leius led off the last of the eighth with a home run to give the Twins a 3-2 win and a 2-0 lead in the series.

Down in Atlanta, in the first World Series ever played in the South, the Braves rallied. In the third the Twins trailed, 4-1, after six innings, but Puckett led off the seventh with a homer, and then in the eighth Chili Davis hit a two-run homer to tie the game. It stay tied until the last of the twelfth, when Mark Lemke singled home David Justice, winning the game. In the fourth game, with the score tied, 2-2, and with one out in the ninth, Lemke tripled and then scored the winning run on a sacrifice fly by Jerry Willard. The series was now tied at two games each, and in the fifth game Atlanta took the lead with a 14-5 victory.

The Twins came home, trailing three games to two, just as in 1965 and 1987. In the sixth game Tapani and Steve Avery hooked up in a good duel. The Twins took a couple of leads but both times Atlanta came back to tie, and the game went

197

into extra-innings. Atlanta manager Bobby Cox brought in left-hander Charlie Leibrandt to pitch in the eleventh—a strange move since Puckett, a right-handed hitter, was leading off. Kirby made them pay for it right away, driving a ball deep to left-center for a game-winning home run.

Once again it all came down to a seventh game. There have been some great seventh games in the World Series, as in 1960, when the Yankees and Pirates battled back and forth, with Pittsburgh winning in the last of the ninth on a home run by Bill Mazeroski. The seventh game between the Twins and Braves was just as exciting. Jack Morris and John Smoltz hooked up in a scoreless duel through seven innings. Then came one of the most incredible innings I've ever seen, even though neither team scored a run. A box score in the newspaper is likely to summarize innings when runs were scored and ignore the scoreless innings, but even though neither team reached home plate in the eighth inning of the seventh game there was some real drama.

Lonnie Smith of Atlanta led off the eighth with a base hit. Terry Pendleton then hit a drive that bounced up the alley in left center field. If the ball had bounced into the seats, it would have been a ground-rule double, and Smith would have to stop at third. The ball stayed in the playing field, however, and it looked as though Smith would easily score the first run of the game. But Smith had trouble picking up sight of the ball after it left Pendleton's bat. Not knowing where it was or if it would be caught, he had to hold up before he got to second. The Twins' infielders went through the motions of fielding a ground ball and throwing to second for a force out. As a result, Smith only reached third, instead of scoring.

Even so, Morris was in trouble since the Braves had runners on second and third with no outs, and the heart of their order was coming up. But Morris got Ron Gant to ground weakly to Hrbek at first. Not only did the Twins get the out, the Atlanta runners had to hold. Justice was intentionally walked to load the bases, set up a force, and bring the less dangerous Sid Bream to the plate. Bream grounded sharply to Hrbek, who threw home to force Smith out at the plate and then hustled to the first-base bag to take the return throw for a double play, ending the inning without allowing a run. Hrbek pumped his arm, and the Metrodome went crazy.

In the last of the eighth the Twins threatened to push a run across. Randy Bush hit a pinch single to start the inning. After Gladden flied out, Chuck Knoblauch singled and the Twins had runners at first and third. That was it for John Smoltz, who was relieved by Mike Stanton. The Braves walked Puckett intentionally. Then Hrbek hit a soft liner up the middle. Second baseman Mark Lemke grabbed it in the air, then stepped on second base to double off Knoblauch and end the inning.

The Twins threatened again in the ninth, getting the first two batters aboard, but Shane Mack grounded into a double play, and, after an intentional walk, Paul Sorrento struck out. The game was still scoreless and headed into extra innings.

Jack Morris was still pitching for the Twins. He had always been a workhorse throughout his career, and with an entire winter to rest up he had no intention of leaving this game. He retired the Braves without any trouble in the tenth.

In the bottom of the inning Dan Gladden broke his bat but dropped a fly ball into short left field. By the time the Braves corralled it, Danny was hustling into second. Chuck Knoblauch laid down a sacrifice bunt to move Gladden to third, with just one out. Puckett and Hrbek were coming up, but both were walked intentionally to load the bases. The

Braves would have to get a double play to end the inning or cut off a run at the plate. They pulled their outfield in because catching a long fly ball would still allow Gladden to score. By playing shallow they might be able to prevent a Texas League hit from falling in and beating them.

Jarvis Brown, who had entered the game in the ninth inning as a pinch runner for designated hitter Chili Davis, was the scheduled batter, but Gene Larkin was sent out to pinch hit. Although Larkin, a switch-hitter batting left against the right-handed Alejandro Pena, wouldn't have to get a hit, he would at least have to make contact. If he did, the Braves were hoping for a ground ball to one of their infielders, so they could turn a double play or force a runner out at home. On the first pitch, Larkin hit a high fly out toward deep left center field. Under normal circumstances, the ball probably would have been caught, although it was deep enough for a runner to tag and score from third. But with the outfielders playing in, left-fielder Brian Hunter didn't have a chance of getting to it.

Gladden, on third, held his base until he saw the ball drop safely, then he started home as the entire Twins' dugout came out to greet him. The first person to meet him after he stepped on the plate with the winning run was Jack Morris, who had just pitched one of the greatest games in the history of the Twins. The scene on the field was even wilder than the celebration in 1987, as the players mobbed both Gladden and Larkin. Then Larkin saw his wife coming onto the field, and he ran over to give her a hug.

There were a lot of heroes of the 1991 season, but Jack Morris was named the World Series Most Valuable Player. Yet 1991 was Morris' only season with the Twins. He was a free agent again and signed with the Toronto Blue Jays. A lot of fans in Minnesota were bitter because they thought that Morris, a Minnesota native, was being disloyal and going elsewhere just because another team was offering more money. But Twins' fans should be thankful for what he did while he was here. The Twins would not have become world champions without him.

In both world championships the Twins won all their home games and lost all their road games, so critics focused on the home-field advantage. Some accused the Twins of shenanigans in the Metrodome, such as the wild accusation that the air fans in the wall behind home plate were turned on when the Twins were at bat, giving their hits a tailwind. Texas manager Bobby Valentine once taped some strips of paper onto the fan grates to show any air currents when the Twins were batting. During the 1987 season the Twins were accused of placing a man behind center field to steal the opposing catcher's signs and signal to the Twins batter what kind of pitch was about to be thrown. Nothing ever came of these accusations. Tim Laudner, who hit .192 in 1987, said, "If we were cheating like that, don't you think I'd be hitting better?"

Such an accusation is not new. In 1965 Jim Landis, who had played eight years for the White Sox before being traded to the Kansas City Athletics, blew the whistle on the White Sox' scoreboard spy. The White Sox accused Landis of sour grapes, saying he was just trying to get back at them for having traded him. But Al Worthington—who was pitching for the Twins at the time Landis made his statements— backed him up. After pitching for the Minneapolis Millers during most of the 1960 season, Worthington had finished out the year with the White Sox. Even though he was in Chicago only a few weeks, he saw first hand what the White Sox were doing with stealing signs. Worthington was so offended by their cheating he let the White Sox know he didn't want to play with them again the next season. He spent the next two seasons in the minors and then played for the Cincinnati Reds in 1963. Later with the Twins he became one of the best relievers in the American League for many years. But from what Al said, it just goes to show you that once in a while there really is something to these types of accusations.

The Game Goes On

The Twins continued their good play through the first half of the 1992 season, and near the end of July they were in first place. Then in a three-game series at the Metrodome the second-place Oakland A's, trailing the Twins by three games, took the first two to pull within a game. Going into the ninth inning of the third game, the Twins had a 5-3 lead, but then Eric Fox of the A's hit a three-run homer off Rick Aguilera, and Oakland won, 6-5. That series was a turning point for both teams. Over the final two months of the season the Twins struggled, while Oakland played exceptionally well and won the division title. That's the last time the Twins have been in a pennant race.

In 1993 they dropped to fifth place, with a record 20 games under .500. That season I missed two and a half months because of my heart surgery. During one of my daily walks at spring training in Fort Myers, Florida, I noticed that my left foot was swollen. I've had a heart murmur all my life, but now one of the valves had started to deteriorate, blood had backed up, and there was fluid retention. Hence the swollen foot. The heart muscle was weakening, and an operation was scheduled for fall, after the baseball season. But around the middle of 1993 my internist Jim Breitenbucher and my cardiologist Norm Chappel decided I shouldn't wait that long. As they explained the surgical procedure and the long period of recuperation, I thought, "I'd rather have to do a month of doubleheaders than go through this."

The surgery to replace a valve in my heart was scheduled for Thursday, July 22. When the Twins went on a road trip a couple weeks before that, I took a break from broadcasting to rest up. On a Tuesday they did an angiogram and found that my arteries were clear. Two days later Dr. Bjorn Monson performed the surgery which went smoothly. I was in the hospital for nine days after the operation and did a few phone interviews on WCCO. I listened to the Twins games on radio and also watched a few on television, since I seldom hear the Twins' television crew. Jim Powell filled in for me on the radio while I was gone. Jim is from Columbia, South Carolina, and had been doing the pregame and postgame shows for the University of South Carolina football. As I listened to the games, I could tell that Jim has a good future in sports announcing.

After I went home and felt stronger, I went to a game at the Metrodome and stopped in the clubhouse. As I was leaving, Tom Kelly walked in. "You mean you had open heart surgery, you had this valve replaced, and you look this good?" he said. "I've got to get one of those."

Originally I was scheduled to resume broadcasting at the beginning of the 1994 season, but I announced the final seven games of the Twins' last home stand of the 1993 season. I felt strong enough before that, but the Twins were on the road, and the doctors advised me not to jump back into the travel routine yet. I was glad to get back into the swing of it to lessen the jolt when the broadcasts began in the next spring.

Overall, I had missed about two-and-a-half months of the season. There were a couple of things I missed out on that I wasn't sorry about, like a 22-inning game against Cleveland in early September. I've had to work a few marathon games like that during my career, and didn't feel at all bad about missing this one. However, there was a moment I would have liked to have been on hand for a couple weeks later. Dave Winfield got his 3,000th career hit, off Dennis Eckersley of Oakland in a game at the Metrodome. It would have been fun to announce that hit, but I had to settle for listening to my longtime partner, John Gordon, describe it on the radio.

Less than a month into the 1994 season, on a Wednesday night game against the Milwaukee Brewers at the Metrodome, Scott Erickson pitched the Twins' first no-hitter in 27 years. Scott had been up and down ever since his 20-win season in 1991 but really had his stuff that night. When Erickson's pitching well, he keeps the ball low and the batters hit a lot of ground balls. On this night he struck out five, got seven batters on fly balls or line drives that were caught, and retired 14 on ground balls (one of those grounders was turned into a double play so the 14 ground balls accounted for 15 outs). In a way, that can show how a pitcher needs to do more than just pitch well to get a no-hitter. He needs some luck, too. With 14 ground balls hit by the Brewers, what are the chances that all of them would be at one of the infielders. Usually, at least a few of those would have found a hole to get through into the outfield. Scott said as much after the game and indicated that in some games in which he gave up a lot of hits, that he really wasn't pitching that poorly. He was giving up ground balls but more than the usual number were getting through the infield. Tonight, the odds evened up in his favor. None got through.

Actually, the two hardest hit balls were by the first two batters of the game. Alex Diaz led off with a well-hit ball caught by Rich Becker in center. Bill Spiers then lined a shot down the third-base line but right at Scott Leius.

The drama really built in the late innings. With one out in

the eighth, Erickson faced Brian Harper, a former Twins' catcher, who had always been a pretty good hitter although never regarded as a top-flight catcher. Some of the pitchers, most notably Erickson, also seemed to have trouble working with him. As a result, the Twins decided to not pick up the option year on Harper's contract after the 1993 season. Brian wasn't too happy about it and probably would have loved to spoil a Twins' no-hit attempt, especially one by Erickson. Scott got two strikes on Harper, but that didn't mean much. Harper had always been a very good two-strike hitter. Harper fouled off a couple pitches to stay alive and increase the tension. Then Erickson pulled the string on his next pitch. Harper had been looking for a fastball and was helpless as a slow curve came in. All he could do was look at it for a called third strike. Erickson had gotten by Harper and then retired John Jaha to finish the eighth.

Scott got the first two batters in the ninth, both on grounders, and the fans were on their feet, stomping and clapping and trying to keep Erickson pumped up for one more out. The Twins had a 6-0 lead, which allowed Erickson to nibble around on the edges of the plate, not giving the batter anything too good. As a result he walked Spiers. He got two strikes on Turner Ward but walked him, too. The next batter was Greg Vaughn, a power hitter who had not looked good in his previous three at-bats. He lifted a fly into short left. For a moment the ball looked as if it might drop in, but left fielder Alex Cole charged in, waving his arms to indicate he had it. Shortstop Pat Meares nearly collided with him, but Cole made the grab, ending the game and completing the no-hitter.

While Erickson was pitching his no-hitter, I refrained from referring directly to it in my announcing. It's not a superstition so much as a tradition, but during the course of a no-hitter I would never say, "Erickson is working on a no-hitter." Some people are critical of that philosophy and feel that I should let listeners know what's going on, but I referred to the Brewers' zeros across the board and commented that the only Milwaukee baserunners were the result of a hit batter and a couple of walks, so it wasn't too hard to figure out.

Ray Christensen came back as a partner for a while in the middle of July. Ray had been scheduled to fill in for me toward the end of the month because I was planning to take some time off, but then he was called to fill in for John Gordon, who was undergoing surgery. Ray was asked on a Monday, and the next day he joined me in Toronto. He had canceled a trip to Colorado Springs to see his son and family because he thought he would be doing the games for the rest of the season. Instead, after a few days the station brought back Jim Powell to finish the season. When Jim filled in for me the year before when I had surgery, he did a good job, but I was disappointed because Ray and I had worked together for four years in the 1970s, and I was looking forward to finishing out the season with him. And Ray had canceled his vacation to Colorado.

On August 4 Kent Hrbek announced that this would be his last season, as many had suspected. That night in a game against the Yankees at the Metrodome he received an ovation when he came to the plate for the first time. He hit a two-run homer off Jim Abbott and received a bigger ovation.

It was a real joy having Herbie on the team all those years. A lot of people say he should have taken better care of himself, that he might have been a Hall of Famer had he been more serious about the game. I think that's unfair. He did a great job both in the field and at the plate for the Twins. His mother, Tina, was his unofficial batting instructor. If he was in a slump, she would call and tell him about some flaw

207

she'd seen in his swing. He loved to talk about the batting tips his mother had given him. The thing I'll always remember about Hrbek is how much fun he had playing baseball. It was a game to him—just like it should be. He was serious about winning, but he was also serious about having a good time and enjoying himself.

A week after Hrbek announced his retirement, on August 12, the season came to a premature end with the players' strike that had been threatening all year. The strike continued into 1995, and spring training was rather bizarre when the owners brought in replacement players to fill in for those on strike. The real players ended their strike and returned to work after a favorable ruling by the National Labor Relations Board, just a few days before the 1995 season was to open. The owners scrapped their plans to start the season with replacement players, and the regular players got into shape with another few weeks of spring training. The Twins opened their season in Boston on April 26, more than three weeks after their scheduled opener.

The strike brought up a lot of issues between the players and owners. In the old days, the players had little say about running the game, although they made attempts to organize even in the 19th century. When Marvin Miller became head of the players' union in the 1960s, the players started making some real gains. In 1975 they were able to eliminate the reserve clause, which bound a player to a particular team for as long as that team wanted him. Even when a player's individual contract expired, he wasn't free to seek employment with another team. Since the end of the reserve clause, the players have been able to offer their talents in an open labor market, leading to a huge increase in salaries. Subsequent labor disputes have been at least indirectly related to the abolition of the reserve clause. In 1981 the players struck for two months when the owners tried to adopt a system in

I joined the on-field ceremony at the 1995 opener when it was
announced that Kent Hrbek's number would be retired.
Linda Schaefer.

Later in the year, I was master or ceremonies for the big day.

My daughter and mother on Christmas in 1985.

Terri attended William & Mary on a golf scholarship.

Terri got married in October of 1994.

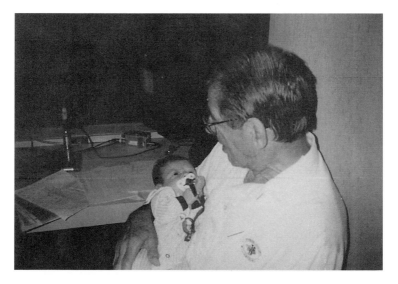

It's never too early to teach them the trade. I brought my new grandson to the broadcast booth when he was a month old.

Kathy and I at our "clubhouse" in Orlando.

which teams who lost a free agent would be compensated by the team signing that player. In 1994 the players went on strike in anticipation of the owners' attempt to implement a salary cap as a means of curbing the escalating payrolls.

When I first became involved with baseball, players stayed with their teams a lot more. Now it's like musical chairs. A guy's with a team for a couple of years, then he's gone somewhere else because of monetary situations. Although Kent Hrbek and Kirby Puckett stayed with the Twins even when they were offered more money by another team, the Twins have lost many good players because they couldn't afford to match offers from other teams. In 1995 the Twins traded away high-salaried players Rick Aguilera, Scott Erickson, and Kevin Tapani in exchange for young prospects who weren't making nearly as much money.

Teams in bigger markets can spend big money on free agents, but the Twins, by developing players through their farm system, won two World Series in five years even though they are a small-market team.

The owners had argued that abolishing the reserve clause would end competitive balance, but the ability to sign a good veteran as a free agent has helped many weak teams improve quickly. After the reserve clause was overturned, in a ten-year period, from 1978 to 1987, there were ten different world champions. That had never happened before. Instead, when the reserve clause was in effect, certain teams dominated their league. From 1921 to 1964 the Yankees won 29 American League pennants. I'd hardly call that competitive balance. On the other hand, players seemed to have more fun before they got the big money.

Another change is that the average time of a game is close to three hours, and now you seldom see a game shorter than two hours. Once in 1973 when Jim Kaat pitched against Bill Singer in California in a game that started at 6:00, the Angels

had scheduled a fireworks show after the game. Both pitchers worked fast and threw strikes. Kaat pitched a one-hitter,
and Singer didn't allow many runners himself. The Twins
won, 2-1, in one hour and 40 minutes. The players show-
ered, dressed, and finally left the ballpark an hour later, and
it still wasn't dark enough to start the fireworks.

I think one reason games are longer these days is that the
umpires have shrunk the strike zone. It's harder for pitchers
to throw strikes, so they tend to go deeper in the count,
adding time to the games. Perhaps the average fan doesn't
care how long a game lasts. But longer games aren't better if
there's nothing going on except one three-ball count after
another. In July 1995 baseball instituted a few changes designed to speed up the pace of the game with more planned
for the 1996 season. I hope they work.

One thing that has not changed much through the years is
the way I prepare for a game. Spring training is a good opportunity to learn about the new players and other information that will last the entire season. Once the season starts, I
spend an average of two hours a day reviewing the players
on both teams. I especially study how the starting pitchers
have done in their last few starts.

Knowing about the pitchers helps to identify their
pitches. From the broadcast booth behind the plate, it's
fairly easy to distinguish a fastball from a breaking pitch.
I've sometimes mistaken a curve ball for a slider, so when
I'm not sure, I call it a breaking ball. But when you know a
pitcher's repertoire, you are better prepared to identify his
pitches.

Baseball isn't rapid-fire like basketball or hockey, and you
need a good supply of material to fill time between pitches.
If there are other games being played at the same time, we
can note their progress. Red Barber, the great announcer for
the Brooklyn Dodgers, said you could never give the score

of your game too often, because people are tuning in all the time. Red used an egg timer to make sure he gave the score every three minutes. I mentioned that on the air once, and a fan sent us an egg timer.

Announcers who cover games that are nationally broadcast should remain neutral, but since I'm the announcer for just one team, I think it's okay to indicate that I'm pulling for the Twins. Although listeners can detect more excitement in my voice when the Twins are doing well, I'm not a cheerleader on the air. Some announcers emphatically root for their team. Bert Wilson of the Cubs used to say, "I don't care who wins as long as it's the Cubs."

Most of my broadcast partners have been announcers trained in the business. Frank Quilici was my only partner who went right from the playing field into the broadcast booth, and he worked hard to learn the techniques of play-by-play. One time when I was sitting in manager Tom Kelly's office before a game, an announcer walked in and started asking questions about the players—was pitcher Allan Anderson right- or left-handed, was Gene Larkin a right- or left-handed batter? This announcer had played some professional baseball and apparently felt that this qualified him to be a broadcaster. Then he turned to Kelly and asked, "How's this Shane Mack playing for you?"

Without even looking up, Kelly said, "Check the stats." If this announcer hadn't done his homework any better than that, Kelly wasn't going to help him.

Many former players have done well, mainly as game analysts on television. Joe Torre, an outstanding major-league catcher as well as manager, was an analyst on California Angels' telecasts for a while. Once before a game, we were chatting about baseball broadcasting, and Joe said, "I couldn't do what you do. Radio play-by-play—it's too hard." On television, the game is on the screen for the viewer to see, whereas on radio, the announcer has to paint a word picture of the action.

Besides spring training and announcing 162 games a season, I have other duties, and most of them are just as much fun as doing play-by-play. A few years ago for the Minnesota Orchestra, I recited Ernest L. Thayer's classic poem "Casey at the Bat" with an elaborate musical accompaniment. During the winter, I'm busy too. I often accompany the Twins caravans around the five-state region when players and front-office members promote the Twins at banquets and community functions.

This kind of thing shows how the running of a baseball team is a year-round operation and also reminds me of how many unsung heroes there are in a baseball team's organization such as Jim Weisner, the Twins' clubhouse manager, and Jim Dunn, who is in charge of the visitors' clubhouse; the media relations people, Rob Antony and his associate, Sean Harlin, along with Wendie Erickson; traveling secretary Remzi Kiratli; and trainers Dick Martin and Doug Nelson. They are a vital part of the team. Tom Mee has worked in media relations more than 30 years and is the official scorer for all games played in the Metrodome.

In January or February, I participate in the Twins' Fantasy Camp in Florida, where fans pay to work out and play some games against teams comprised of former Twins. I broadcast these games and have a great time with former Twins like Killebrew and Battey while Kathy renews friendships with some of the wives.

Kathy and I now spend our winters in Florida, at our Winter Garden house from the end of November until mid-February and then at our Fort Myers condominium, where we can watch the sunset over the Gulf of Mexico. When we first moved to Florida for the winter, our daughter, Terri, attended school there for that semester. At first we were concerned that uprooting her might interfere with her studies, but her schoolwork didn't suffer, and she was on the boys' golf team at West Orange High School, playing a lot more golf than would have been possible in Minnesota in the winter.

Terri graduated from Eisenhower High in Hopkins, Minnesota, in 1981. One of her golf teammates was Jody Rosenthal, who went on to play at the University of Tulsa and then on the pro golf tour, where she was named Rookie of the Year in the Ladies' Professional Golf Association. Terri had some scholarship offers to play golf at several schools, and she chose William and Mary, in Williamsburg, Virginia. Terri did well there and was named Woman Athlete of the Year when she was a junior. She gave some thought to joining Jody on the pro golf tour, but she decided to play golf just for fun. She married Dick Doll in October 1994, and their son, Matthew Charles, was born on July 12, 1995.

As for me, I think I'd have trouble giving up announcing completely. I'm like my old partner, Ray Christensen, who's still going strong as the voice of the Minnesota Gophers. I want to keep going as long as the fans want to listen to me.

Appendix:
Hot Stove Time

Baseball lends itself not only to radio but to stories. For some reason there are many more anecdotes about baseball than any other sport. Dave Moore of WCCO Television often asks, "When's the last time you heard a good hockey story?"

One of my favorite baseball stories concerns Gaylord Perry, who won more than 300 games and was the only pitcher to win the Cy Young Award in both the American and National leagues. When he came over to the American League in the early 1970s, Gaylord was known for his spitball, certainly not his hitting. Of course, during later years in the American League he didn't have to bat because of the designated-hitter rule, but when he started his career in the early 1960s with the San Francisco Giants, he had to take his cuts like everyone else. His manager with the Giants, Alvin Dark, once said, "The day Gaylord Perry hits a home run, they'll put a man on the moon." Gaylord Perry hit his first major-league home run on Sunday, July 20, 1969. That's right—the day the first men landed on the moon.

Many of my favorite stories I heard from Al Lopez, who had a good career as a catcher in the majors and then became a very successful manager. When Al was managing the Chicago White Sox in the 1960s, he told me about the time the Brooklyn Dodgers were managed by Burleigh Grimes, from Clear Lake, Wisconsin. Burleigh was a great pitcher and the last to throw a legal spitball. Burleigh was elected to the Hall of Fame in 1964, but when he managed the Dodgers, the team wasn't very good. Once, in a game against the Cubs, Burleigh got into an argument with an umpire and was thrown out of the game. At that time a team had few coaches and the manager usually served as the third-base coach. When Burleigh got thrown out, Andy High, who usually coached first, moved into the third-base coaching box, and Max Butcher, a pitcher not playing that day, filled in as first-base coach.

The Dodgers were trailing, 8-1, in the top of the ninth, when Gibby Brack, an outfielder, led off the inning with a single. To signal for a steal, Andy High would wink several times. Of course, in this case, down by seven runs, the Dodgers weren't likely to take chances off the bases. But filling in as first-base coach made Max Butcher nervous, and he developed a tic, blinking an eye. Gibby, the runner at first, was astonished that Butcher was giving him the sign to steal, but he took off for second and was thrown out easily.

In the clubhouse after the game, Burleigh Grimes yelled at Brack, "What were you doing trying to steal when we're seven runs down?"

"It wasn't my idea," Gibby said. "Max was coaching at first and gave me the steal sign."

"I don't believe it."

Burleigh stormed over toward Butcher. Seeing his manager on the warpath and heading his way, Butcher had another attack of nerves and started blinking his eye again.

Brack, who was following Grimes, said, "Hey, look, Burleigh—he's giving it to me again!"

Another story of a player in an unfamiliar position involved Frankie Skaff, a native of LaCrosse, Wisconsin, when he was managing Ottawa in the International League. In a game against the Rochester Red Wings, the Ottawa first baseman was hurt, so Skaff, the manager, moved Stan Jok from his usual third-base position over to first. Rochester had a runner on first with no outs, when the batter bunted down the first-base line. Jok charged in, fielded the ball, and tried to tag the batter, but the batter ran back toward home plate. Jok threw the ball to catcher Neil Wattlington, and they had the batter in a rundown between home and first. By the time they tagged him out, the runner on first had advanced all the way to third. Rochester won the game.

Afterward in the clubhouse, Skaff asked Jok, "What in the world were you thinking about? Why didn't you just go step on first base to put that batter out? That way we could have held the other runner at second."

"Well, I forgot I was playing first base," Stan said. "I thought I was still playing third and we had the guy in a rundown between home and third."

Skaff turned to Wattlington and said, "What did you think you were doing on that play?"

Wattlington replied, "I didn't understand it myself, but I figured Stan is a pretty smart guy and knew what he was doing, so I just kept going with it until we got the guy out."

Al Lopez remembers another story about when he was catching for the Boston Braves, and the team's second baseman was Tony Cuccinello. Cuccinello was thrown out trying to go from first to third on a single. He had gone into third standing up, despite a signal from the third-base coach to slide. Afterward Lopez asked him why he didn't slide.

"I couldn't slide," Cuccinello said.

"What do you mean, you couldn't slide?"

"I had all my cigars in my hip pocket."

When Al was managing the Chicago White Sox, one of the team's better minor-league prospects was brought up toward the end of the season. He wasn't going to play much, but the White Sox thought they'd let him soak up a little major-league atmosphere. The kid was really eager to learn. During games he'd sit next to Lopez in the dugout during games and try to learn as much as he could. In a game against the Yankees, Nellie Fox, the White Sox second baseman, got a hit in the fourth inning. The next batter also singled down the right-field line and Fox tried to go to third. Roger Maris, playing right field for the Yankees, raced over, grabbed the ball on one bounce, and made a tremendous throw to third to nail Fox.

"Mr. Lopez, was that the right play for Mr. Fox to go from first to third?" the kid phenom asked.

"Son, it was absolutely the right play," Lopez said. "Roger Maris couldn't make another throw like that in a hundred years."

A few innings later Fox singled again. The next batter singled to right, and Maris scooped up the ball, and made another great throw to get Fox at third again.

The White Sox dugout was stunned. Finally the kid said, "Golly, Mr. Lopez, up here in the big leagues time sure does fly."

Another storyteller I enjoy visiting is Angelo Giuliani, a former catcher, a former scout for the Twins, and the man who was largely responsible for starting the Twins' baseball clinics. Angie was the catcher for the St. Louis Browns when the team was managed by Rogers Hornsby, one of the outstanding hitters of all time. Annoyed whenever a pitcher gave up a hit after getting two strikes on a batter, especially if he was ahead in the count, Hornsby instituted a $25 fine for any pitcher who threw a strike when the count was 0-2. Once when Angie was catching, a left-hander named Jim Walkup got an 0-2 count on the batter. Angie signaled for a curve ball in the dirt. Walkup threw a curve, but it came in right over the plate, just above the batter's knees.

The umpire called, "Strike Three!"

Walkup, realizing he was about to lose $25, charged in and hollered, "C'mon Ump. That pitch was low!"

A few years later Angie was with the Senators when they had Joe Krakauskas, a strong left-hander, who could throw hard but not always accurately. One day at Yankee Stadium the starting pitcher was in a jam, so manager Bucky Harris sent word to the bullpen for Krakauskas to start warming up. After a couple more Yankee hits, Harris asked one of his players if Krakauskas was ready yet. The player looked at the bullpen and saw Krakauskas let loose with a wild warm-up pitch that sailed over the bullpen's eight-foot-high gate and onto the playing field. The player said to Harris, "He's ready!"

As a rule, players or managers aren't thrown out of games in spring training. But I remember one incident when the Twins were playing an exhibition game against the Philadelphia Phillies in Clearwater, Florida. We'd heard that the Phillies' manager at that time, Gene Mauch, had been ejected from a game the day before by umpire Ed Hurley. By chance, Hurley's crew was on hand for the game that day in Clearwater. With the start of the game just minutes away the managers brought out their line of cards for the umpires at home place. Before long we noticed that Mauch was getting into a rather animated discussion with Hurley, and Hurley eventually told Gene to leave the premises. I'm sure that that's a spring training record—not only being ejected two games in a row in exhibition games, but the second time before the game even started.

The shortest term for any manager was one game. In 1977 the Texas Rangers fired Frank Lucchesi as their manager and hired Eddie Stanky while the Rangers were in Minnesota for a series against the Twins at Metropolitan Stadium. Stanky had managed teams in the majors and minors, including the Millers in 1956 when they played the first game in the history of Met Stadium. Now with Stanky as their new manager, the Rangers beat the Twins, but back at the hotel that night Stanky decided he wanted to go home to his family and look after his aging parents. So the next morning he resigned and went home. Texas then promoted coach Connie Ryan to interim manager, and within a day they hired Billy Hunter to manage the team the rest of the season. That's four managers within four days—a record that even the Yankees' George Steinbrenner hasn't approached. The best Steinbrenner could do was three managers in one season: Bob Lemon, Gene Michael, and Clyde King in 1982.

Eddie Stanky had quite a career as a player. When Stanky was playing for the Giants, Branch Rickey of the Dodgers said of him, "He can't hit, can't run, can't throw, can't field. All he can do is beat you." Stanky was a second baseman who would do anything to help his team win. In a crucial situation he often jumped up and down, trying to distract the batter, before that practice was outlawed. Away from the ballpark Stanky was the most pleasant guy you could ever meet, but once he put his uniform on, either as a player or a manager, he sprouted horns.

One record no pitcher wants to beat belongs to Twins' right-hander Terry Felton, who lost 16 games in a row. His major-league career began in 1980, and he had a career record of 0-3 coming into the 1982 season. Felton lost 13 games without a win in 1982, and that was it for him, finishing with a lifetime record of 0-16.

Once in a home game against Oakland Felton was sent in around the fifth or sixth inning. The sports ticker that sent information about out-of-town games to stadiums across the country had mistakenly identified him as the starting pitcher, so when the ticker reported that Felton was coming into the game in relief for the Twins, the Royals' announcer in Kansas City, Fred White, said, "Well, fans, it seems that up in Minnesota, Terry Felton has just relieved himself on the mound."

A questionable pitch can ignite a bench-clearing brawl. Usually it's a pushing and shoving contest, but some brawls are rough. One of the worst I ever saw was at Metropolitan Stadium when Twins' right-hander Ray Corbin beaned Bob Coluccio of the Brewers. Coluccio took a couple of steps toward the mound and collapsed in front of the plate. Players poured out of both dugouts. Some Brewers headed for Corbin while others ran over to check Coluccio's condition. The big Milwaukee first baseman George "Boomer" Scott went after Twins manager Frank Quilici because he thought Frank had ordered Corbin to throw at Coluccio. Corbin was dragged toward the Brews' dugout and given a pretty good going over.

A less explosive incident occurred in 1969 when the Twins' Dick Woodson, not noted for control, threw two consecutive high inside pitches at Reggie Jackson, who had hit two homers earlier in the game. After the second pitch Jackson charged at Woodson and tried to tackle him, but Woodson, who stood about six foot six, did not go down, and Reggie didn't know what to do next. That was the end of that confrontation. Jackson and Woodson later became friends.

In a similar incident Jack McDowell of the White Sox low-bridged the Blue Jay's Mark Whiten, who charged the mound. McDowell stood his ground, and Whiten pounded him on the jaw. Later somebody asked McDowell, "Why didn't you try to defend yourself?"

"Well," McDowell said, "when those batters come after the pitcher, I thought they only tackled them."

Sometimes the "purpose pitch" backfires. In a game at California, Dean Chance of the Twins thought that the California pitcher Sammy Ellis had been throwing at some of the Twins, so when Ellis came up to bat, Chance plunked him in the ribs. By making a base runner out of the Angels' pitcher, however, Chance had put the winning run on base, and the Angels won the game, 2-1.

Wayne Terwilliger, a former Twins' coach, tells of the time that he was playing with the Chicago Cubs against the Philadelphia Phillies and facing their right-hander Robin Roberts, one of the greatest control pitchers of all time. Twig was not a big hitter. Generally, when he had a count of three balls and no strikes, he was told not swing at the next pitch, but this time he got the green light to swing. The next pitch was a fastball down the middle. Twig took a mighty swing but just fouled it off. The next pitch hit Terwilliger right in the ribs. As he was going to first base, Robin Roberts yelled at him, "You little twerp, don't you ever swing at me on three-and-oh again!"

When I was growing up in Richmond, Cardinal outfielder Joe "Ducky" Medwick was one of my favorite players. Many years later when I was broadcasting with the Twins, I met Lefty Heise, who had played for the Cardinals with Joe Medwick. Lefty told me, "Joe never lacked for confidence, and when he was in the minor leagues, you could tell that it was only a matter of time before he became an outstanding major-league hitter."

Medwick was a notoriously bad ball hitter, though, and Lefty said he often swung at pitches way out of the strike zone—and connected for line drives. In one exhibition game against the Yankees, with Bill Dickey catching for New York, a pitch came in well over Medwick's head, but he lined the ball into left center field for a double. Afterward when the players were talking about Medwick's incredible hit catcher Bill Dickey said, "If Medwick hadn't hit that ball, there was no way I was going to catch it."

Medwick was also called Muscles because he was a very strong player. Once he misplayed a ball in the outfield, and when the team returned to the dugout at the end of the inning, the pitcher, Ed Heusser, said, "It's too bad Medwick can't catch a fly ball." Medwick belted him on the jaw and knocked him out cold.

When Medwick went up to the big leagues, the opposing pitchers knew of his reputation as a bad-ball hitter, but they thought they could intimidate him by throwing head-high fastballs. Medwick would either duck the pitch or step back and line the ball for an extra base hit. One time, when a couple of pitches had almost beheaded Medwick, he still came up with a hit. Back in the dugout he said, "These guys up here in the big leagues are a lot wilder than they are in the minor leagues."

I've been fortunate to meet many of the great players, as well as many of the great characters, associated with baseball, and to share in some of their stories.

Index